SINGAPORE
PERSPECTIVES
2011
Our Inclusive Society: Going Forward

SINGAPORE
PERSPECTIVES
2011
Our Inclusive Society: Going Forward

Edited by

Faizal bin Yahya

Lee Kuan Yew
School of Public Policy
National University of Singapore

iPS Institute of
Policy Studies

World Scientific

Published by

World Scientific Publishing Co. Pte. Ltd.

5 Toh Tuck Link, Singapore 596224

USA office: 27 Warren Street, Suite 401-402, Hackensack, NJ 07601

UK office: 57 Shelton Street, Covent Garden, London WC2H 9HE

British Library Cataloguing-in-Publication Data
A catalogue record for this book is available from the British Library.

SINGAPORE PERSPECTIVES 2011
Our Inclusive Society: Going Forward

ISBN-13 978-981-4374-56-9 (pbk)
ISBN-10 981-4374-56-3 (pbk)

In-house Editor: Sandhya Venkatesh

Printed in Singapore.

Contents

Foreword

When the themes for Singapore Perspectives 2011 were initially mooted, greater attention was placed on the economy and related issues. However, as we debated the key points this annual flagship conference should focus on, it became clear that our society has been significantly affected by the relentless pursuit of economic growth.

For example, the influx of foreign talent has not only raised questions about "bread and butter" issues, but also Singaporeans' perception of national identity and sense of belonging. Singapore Perspectives 2011 was, therefore, an opportune moment to take stock of the health of Singapore's society in the wake of intense globalisation, and to attempt a prognosis of its future.

The constant requirement in organising Singapore Perspectives is to put together a slate of good speakers, with interesting viewpoints and ideas that will inspire and provoke the participants of the conference. At the same time, a balance is needed, as the occasion is also a review of recent events and how Singaporeans have measured up to new expectations and ensuing policies. Indeed, the ground that has to be covered is often too extensive, even when a deliberate narrowing of focus has been done and competing interests have been properly prioritised. Another goal for the conference is to stimulate interactive exchanges between the participants. The challenge is to overcome the reticence of the audience and the fatigue of a day-long event.

I hope that the team responsible for Singapore Perspectives 2011 has lived up to the expectations of the ardent supporters of the Institute of Policy Studies. The most important thing is that we learn from our shortcomings to improve the future editions of the conference. In this respect, we value feedback and suggestions from everyone who attended Singapore Perspectives 2011.

ONG KENG YONG
Former Director
Institute of Policy Studies

Acknowledgements

IPS is grateful to the following institutions for their support of Singapore Perspectives 2011 held on Monday, 17 January 2011.

Made possible by

Keppel Corporation

**TEMASEK
HOLDINGS**

Supported by

HILL & KNOWLTON

HOUSING &
DEVELOPMENT
BOARD

ITE
Institute of Technical Education

Jardine Cycle & Carriage

KPMG

M P A
SINGAPORE

NYP Nanyang
Polytechnic

NANYANG
TECHNOLOGICAL
UNIVERSITY

NUS
National University
of Singapore

NGEE ANN
POLYTECHNIC

Supported by

PHILIPS

REPUBLIC
POLYTECHNIC

SHELL
CELEBRATES
120 YEARS IN
SINGAPORE
1891–2011
SHAPING OUR FUTURE TODAY

SIM
UNIVERSITY

SMU
SINGAPORE MANAGEMENT
UNIVERSITY

SINGAPORE
POLYTECHNIC

SMRT

TEMASEK
POLYTECHNIC

Editor's Acknowledgements

We would like to thank all the authors in this volume for their patience and understanding in working towards the production of this publication. The papers in this volume reflect variety of writing styles and views from a very diverse group of panelists and it was quite a task to provide "value-added" comments. Nonetheless, the panelists responded positively to editors' comments. Given the unique composition of the panelists, we have included the responses of the discussants to provide additional insights into the issues.

From IPS, I would like to thank Tan Simin and Tan Tarn How in providing advice in the preparation of this manuscript, Rachel Hui and Sarjune Ibrahim for proof reading the manuscript, and Joanne Low for coordinating with the copy editor. I would like to also thank Gillian Koh for coordinating the publication of the manuscript and last but not least Director Ong Keng Yong for his advice and encouragement in the publication of this volume.

Faizal bin Yahya

I

Our Inclusive Society: Going Forward

Conference Concept

Singapore is well-known for beating the odds. Turning adversities into opportunities, Singapore's rapid growth and success has won over critics and gained admirers. With practicality, pragmatism, and innovation, it has found solutions to the unique challenges faced by the country. Singaporeans pride themselves on being part of a meritocratic society, with an exemplary government plugged into the international grid.

However, Singapore remains dependent on the global economy for its success and survival. Rapid growth has also led to a growing number of disparities that threaten to undermine social cohesion and the aspiration for an inclusive society.

Singapore Perspectives 2011, the annual flagship Conference of the Institute of Policy Studies (IPS), seeks to examine the challenges ahead, and ways to effectively handle them. In particular, the Conference considers the policy innovations necessary for the future. The theme of the this year's Conference was "Our Inclusive Society: Going Forward." Three panels of speakers and discussants deliberated the issues relevant to these topics — "Global City," "Caring Community," and "Singapore Spirit."

Welcome Remarks

ONG KENG YONG
Monday 17 January 2011
Raffles City Convention Centre

I am pleased to welcome Deputy Prime Minister Wong Kan Seng, distinguished guests, friends, ladies and gentlemen to the 2011 Singapore Perspectives Conference. This is the Institute's flagship event. It started in the year 2000.

Since then, many policy-makers and experts have spoken at the Singapore Perspectives Conferences. This year, we are honoured to have Deputy Prime Minister Wong to deliver the Keynote Address. Thank you, Deputy Prime Minister Wong, for spending time with us this morning.

Today, we have an exciting line-up of panelists and speakers, who will discuss and exchange views on issues that relate to the Conference's theme — "Our Inclusive Society: Going Forward".

When we first began conceptualising the theme of this year's Conference, we wanted to study the recommendations of the Economic Strategies Committee (ESC), which convened in 2009 to develop strategies for restructuring the national economy. However, subsequent developments made it clear that Singaporeans were interested in a wider variety of issues, such as inclusive growth, social mobility and the future of Singapore.

Developing the theme of the Conference, there are three panels and they will dwell on the "Global City," "Caring Community," and "Singapore Spirit" respectively. There will also be a Special Session to discuss how these three topics interacted with each other and brought about the desired results.

Singapore Perspectives Conference has always aimed to draw out views and ideas from as wide a spectrum of society as possible. We hope you will find the speakers' perspectives thought-provoking and engaging. Please feel free to comment and ask questions, so that this will be a worthwhile experience for you.

We hope you will find today's programme rewarding, and that you will feel inspired and educated when you leave the Conference at the end of the day.

We received strong support from the statutory boards, institutions of higher learning and outstanding private-sector companies for this event. Singapore Perspectives Conferences would not have been possible without their continuous support. I would like to make a special mention of Keppel Corporation and Temasek Holdings, both of which have made many IPS activities possible. IPS looks forward to many more years of cooperation with all the sponsors.

Keynote Address

DEPUTY PRIME MINISTER MR WONG KAN SENG
AND COORDINATING MINISTER FOR NATIONAL
SECURITY

Introduction

It gives me great pleasure to be present for this year's Singapore Perspectives Conference.

The theme for this year's conference is "Our Inclusive Society: Going Forward." There are panels discussing the three sub-themes — Global City, Caring Society, and the Singapore Spirit. It is timely and important for the Conference to address these issues.

It is timely, because our economy has just recovered strongly, growing by 14.7% in 2010, after a recession in 2009. We are not likely to see such stellar growth for a long time to come. We should take stock of what we did well. Going forward, we must continue with sound policies to help us tackle the challenges of this fast-changing world.

It is important, because inclusiveness and cohesion have always been the cornerstones of our multi-racial and multi-religious society because it is vital for us to preserve what works, and what is unique and precious about our society.

Part 1: Global City, Endearing Home

Our economy recovered strongly last year due to improved global economic conditions, which were the result of government intervention worldwide. The Singapore Government also took swift measures to deal with the economic problems head-on. The Resilience Package announced during the

2009 Budget helped both companies and workers. In order to sustain our development and deliver a better life to Singaporeans, we must continue to be open and connected so as to grow our economy.

Our rapid recovery was also possible due to the ongoing improvements to our economic fundamentals. Over the last ten years, we have made great strides towards becoming a global city and society. We have attracted many international players in industries such as pharmaceuticals, biotechnology, alternative energy, aerospace engineering, and tourism. We have broadened and deepened the base of our economy.

The developments around Marina Bay have created one of the most striking downtown landscapes in the world. We now have a beautiful skyline around a state-of-the-art barrage. Our residential heartlands are also being remade and rejuvenated. Looking ahead, Singapore will only become a more exciting place for residents and visitors alike, when upcoming attractions such as the Gardens by the Bay, the River Safari, the National Art Gallery, and the Sports Hub are completed.

Our voice is heard in international forums and taken seriously only because we are successful. If we are not, then no one will pay attention to us. According to a study by *Foreign Policy* magazine, consulting firm A.T. Kearney and The Chicago Council, Singapore is one of the top ten global cities in the world in terms of how much influence it has on what happens beyond its borders, and how well it interacts with global markets, culture, and innovation.

Not all Singaporeans are comfortable with the pace of change and development. I can understand why, and I empathise with them. Some point out that the pace of life has picked up so fast that they are experiencing higher levels of stress. Some attribute the problems related to congestion and increased prices to the presence of many foreigners, and feel that we should admit fewer of them. Others are concerned about the potential erosion of our Singaporean identity, as we grow and become more cosmopolitan. In short, Singaporeans wonder whether a global city can also be an endearing home.

For Singapore, becoming a global city is not merely an aspiration. It is a pre-requisite for our survival. Being open is the only viable option for us if we wish to be self-reliant and continue to prosper. Closing our doors will only turn us into an island of no consequence, unable to provide for our people and becoming irrelevant to the world.

Being open allows us to connect and trade with the rest of the world, and, in doing so, attract the best investments and talents to Singapore. Being open also helps us to overcome our physical constraints and small population. It helps us to create great things from the little things that we have. This is how, for example, despite having zero oil production, we became a global leader in oil trading, oil refining, oil-rig building, and so on. Singapore companies such as Singapore Airlines and Neptune Orient Lines are among the leaders in global transportation, despite Singapore being just an island of 710 sq km.

Nearly 40 years ago, the late Mr S. Rajaratnam had summed it up succinctly in 1972. He said: "If you view Singapore's future not as a regional city but as a Global City, then the smallness of Singapore, the absence of a hinterland, raw materials, and a large domestic market are not fatal or insurmountable handicaps. It would explain why, since independence, we have been successful economically and consequently, and have ensured political and social stability."

At the same time, Singapore has to be more than just a global city. More than anything else, this is our home, a place where we belong. Other global cities such as New York, London, Tokyo, and Hong Kong, are part of far larger countries. They are connected to wider hinterlands that provide a constant source of skills and labour to sustain their competitiveness. Also, people in these cities can opt to move out of the city to another part of the same country for a more leisurely pace of life, lower costs of living, or to simply take a break from the hustle and bustle of a big, urbanised city.

As a small city-state, we are not like New York, London, or Tokyo. Our city is also our country and our home. To be an endearing home as well as a global city, we have to resolve a few tensions. One has to do with size, and the other has to do with change.

Most global cities have sizeable populations. New York, London, Tokyo, and Hong Kong all have populations of between seven to nine million people. Many aspiring global cities, like Shanghai, have even larger populations. While population size is not everything, it does provide a critical mass for attracting investors and growing domestic markets.

Singapore, however, is a compact city-state, and any growth in population size must be balanced against the need to maintain a liveable environment and a harmonious ambience. Because we are severely constrained in land area, we do what we can to create more land through reclamation, and building upwards and even underground. But there are limits. This is the first tension that we have to resolve.

Global cities are also centres of change, as they are open to constant flows of people, capital, technology, and ideas. To thrive, global cities like us remake themselves from time to time, implementing bold initiatives that the rest of the world study eventually adopt. NEWater, the Electronic Road Pricing system, and our extensive and successful public housing programme are but a handful of our pioneering innovations which have attracted many overseas study delegations.

Too much change may lead to the risk of losing the essence of home. Home is about familiarity, stability, and comfort. We want to retain the vibrancy and dynamism of a city on the move, without eroding the sense of belonging and pride in our shared heritage. This is the second tension that has to be resolved.

Part 2: Our Way Forward

Resolving these tensions of size and change will be tough, but not impossible. These are the challenges that will drive and shape the work of the newly inaugurated National Population and Talent Division (NPTD). The NPTD's key function is to formulate, coordinate, and review whole-of-government policies related to population and talent. It will focus on achieving a sustainable population profile. Ultimately, it is about navigating a path that allows us to grow as a global city, while remaining as a distinctive and endearing home.

In doing so, the NPTD, along with other government departments and agencies, will be guided by three key principles. First, we have to preserve and uphold what is distinctive and unique about Singapore. Second, we will ensure that growth and change benefit Singaporeans. Third, we will remain nimble and be prepared to make adjustments along the way.

Preserve what is unique about Singapore

The first principle is to retain and preserve what is unique and distinct about Singapore.

To some, what makes Singapore unique or distinct is the presence of friends and family, and the treasured memories of time spent growing up in Singapore. To others, it could be our unique food culture, or just simply our way of life. To Singaporean men, it is the memorable experience of National Service, which has instilled a deep sense of why we must defend our country.

To me, what is distinctive and unique about Singapore boils down to two aspects. One is our national character, which has been shaped by our forefathers and by our journey in nation-building. Being descendants of immigrants who had to make their livings on unfamiliar shores, we value hard work, thrift, and honesty. This is the basis of our meritocratic society. Despite living in a highly urbanised environment, many of us still subscribe to the *gotong royong* spirit of neighbourliness and mutual assistance. We can be competitive, or *kiasu*, but we also have a strong tradition of philanthropy, volunteerism, and caring for one another. We saw these qualities in the early years, when migrants came to Singapore and extended help to one another.

We are an orderly, law-abiding people, but not so serious that we cannot poke fun at ourselves with a humour that is folksy and unpretentious. But no matter how much better life has become for us, all true-blue Singaporeans will readily sit down at a hawker centre table and heartily enjoy the same hawker food that nourished our forefathers decades ago. Our habits and character as people reflect the simplicity of our roots.

Second is our multi-ethnic, multi-religious, and multi-lingual society. Our forefathers came mainly from Asia, and some from other parts of the world. Our diverse roots and decades of living together helped us to understand the importance of tolerance, harmony, and unity, all of which have been painstakingly fostered and nurtured over the years. This is a unique feature of Singapore, which we must treasure.

Even rarer is the fact that we have made this diversity work for us. Most of us are so used to this that we do not even think of it as unusual. It has

9

become part of our DNA. But to casual visitors, this is an achievement that they truly marvel at and admire.

Let me quote from Mr Jack Blaylock, a frequent visitor to Singapore, who made the following observation in a letter to *The Straits Times Forum* recently: "On a daily basis, I see Christian, Muslim, and Hindu office-workers sharing meals at a *kopitiam* (coffee shop), exchanging smiles or pleasantries on the street or otherwise kindly extending help to one another. In all my trips here, I have not once witnessed religion-fuelled hostility or prejudice. My travels have taken me to all corners of the world, yet I have never found a country that comes even close to the religious and spiritual maturity that Singaporeans demonstrate towards one another."

Our people and our multi-ethnic society makes Singapore distinct. This is why, in managing our population, we are always guided by the need to preserve a strong citizen core, and to maintain stability in our ethnic mix. A sustainable population profile must be able to address both needs.

Ensuring that growth and change benefits Singaporeans

The second principle is to ensure that any growth and change is for the benefit of Singaporeans.

One tangible benefit of our progress towards becoming a global city is our increased links with the rest of the world. As we grow, there will be an increase in job opportunities. The strong economic growth last year corresponded with low unemployment rates. Singapore's unemployment rate fell to 2.1% in the third quarter of 2010, the lowest level in two and a half years.

While growth in 2011 is unlikely to be as exceptional as in 2010, there will continue to be many job opportunities available for Singaporeans. There are many measures in place for Singaporeans to upgrade their skills. This will allow them to move into better and more productive jobs and earn higher wages over time.

Jobs, however, are not the only benefits enjoyed by Singaporeans. With economic growth, there are also more choices and options for enriching our lives. Today, we see services or products that would have been considered niche 20 years ago. As recently as ten years ago, the Esplanade, which is a world-class theatre and performance venue, did not exist. The local food and beverage (F&B) scene was significantly less vibrant. For example, popular F&B enclave Dempsey Hill, a disused Army barracks, had not yet been developed. For many, especially younger Singaporeans, it may be hard to imagine what life would be without access to these choices and options.

Even in essential areas such as education, economic growth has expanded our choices. We have now developed more pathways beyond the "O" Levels and for students to achieve their full potential. Those who are athletic and have a passion for sports can choose to hone their abilities at the Singapore Sports School. The artistic ones have a chance to nurture their talent at the new School of the Arts. They do not have to leave home to pursue these interests.

The Government has pledged that Singaporeans' interest comes first. We will continue to ensure that any growth and change is for the benefit of Singaporeans. Part of that involves allowing a sufficient intake of foreign manpower to top up our local workforce in order to meet economic needs. Ultimately, by making Singapore attractive to employers and investors, we will ensure that good jobs will remain in Singapore, for Singaporeans. At the same time, we will ensure that our population strategy mitigates the impact of ageing, so that the gains from economic growth will not be significantly reduced by the additional social burden of an increasingly ageing society.

Ensuring sufficient manpower for economic growth and mitigating the impact of ageing are two other needs that must be managed in achieving a sustainable population profile for Singapore.

The key hurdle to achieving a sustainable population lies in our local fertility rate, which is quite weak. For more than 30 years, we have not been having enough babies to replace ourselves. Preliminary estimates indicate that our resident total fertility rate has fallen to 1.16 in 2010, even lower than the 1.22 in 2009. The going is hard, but we have not given up. We will continue to support couples' decisions to get married and have children, and aim to create a pro-family environment. To be realistic, however, we must accept that boosting fertility will take a long time. For the foreseeable future, we will need to tap on immigration to augment our population, to support economic growth, and to mitigate the impact of ageing.

Being prepared to make adjustments

The third principle, ladies and gentlemen, is to stay nimble and be ready to make adjustments along the way. We will continue to monitor the impact of our population policies closely and introduce refinements as and when necessary, to ensure that the policy initiatives serve the needs of a sustainable population.

We have already tightened the immigration framework to better manage the inflow and quality of new immigrants in the last quarter of 2009. As a result, the number of new permanent residences granted has fallen — from 59,460 in 2009, to 29,265 in 2010. We have observed an improvement in the quality of new permanent residents (PRs). Because we have been able to attract new citizens of good quality, the number of new citizenships granted has remained relatively stable at 19,928 in 2009 and 18,758 in 2010.

We have also drawn sharper distinctions between the benefits available to Singaporeans, PRs, and other foreigners, in areas such as housing, education, and healthcare. This underlines our principle that Singaporeans will enjoy priority over non-citizens.

Ladies and Gentlemen, Singapore's population story is still evolving. Looking ahead, continual refinements will need to be made at appropriate junctures to ensure that Singapore will remain our best home. Like other countries around the world, we must continue to welcome suitably qualified people to work and live in Singapore, and contribute to our society.

Conclusion

Before I conclude, let me sum up. While the drive towards becoming a global city and our quest to remain as an endearing home for Singaporeans may pull us in different directions, resolving them is not impossible. Our "can-do" Singapore Spirit will help us overcome the challenges before us. We will continue to forge our own path, by preserving what is unique and distinct about Singapore, and by being nimble and adaptable.

Whatever we do, we will ensure that Singaporeans will benefit from growth and change. The benefits will be concrete. We will not leave behind those who need more help. The surpluses we have set aside in good times can be tapped on to look after the needs of the poor and the old.

Singaporeans will continue to enjoy quality education, healthcare, transport, and other social infrastructure.

Our lives will get better as we continue to work hard and remain competitive. This is the Singapore that we have built and will continue to improve — a country that provides the best home for all Singaporeans and creates bright opportunities for future generations. A home where we can enjoy, what the rest of the world offers, and still remain firmly rooted with our Singaporean family and friends.

I wish you all a fruitful discussion today. Thank you.

II

Global City

Singapore has been a global city since its inception in 1819. It was established to play a crucial role in cross-region commerce, with human capital comprising diverse groups of people. Today, enhanced talent flow and Singapore's established position on the world map present many challenges for the continued functioning and flourishing of this global city. How can we continue to attract talented professionals and make Singapore a home for them, rather than a mere stopover? At the same time, how do we develop human resources suitable for the needs of the changing global landscape? Increased globalisation and the necessary talent policies — including the Permanent Resident scheme — have also resulted in a more diverse population in terms of outlook and aspirations. How do we maintain social order without sacrificing the creative energies of these varied groups? How should home-grown Singaporeans cope with increased competition for education, employment, and other spaces? Given Singapore's size and global reach, Singapore should perhaps be thought of as a "global state" rather than a global city. What are the regional and international roles Singapore can play as an open and connected hub?

CHAPTER 1

Between Nation-State and Global City

DEREK DA CUNHA

This paper will examine the following themes:

- Between nation-state and global city
- Monaco of the East?
- The bet on casinos
- A diversified economy
- Opinions and practices in a global city

BETWEEN NATION-STATE AND GLOBAL CITY

The concept of the global city is often viewed in economic terms. Its simple definition is that it is a city that is an important nodal point in the global economic system. To that extent, there are several international surveys that rank many cities or countries in terms of their levels of globalisation. These rankings are based largely on economic, political, cultural, and infrastructural characteristics.

The global management consultancy, A. T. Kearney, in its 2006 rankings, rated Singapore the most globalised country in the world.[1] Note the word "country," not "city." This is the main problem with these surveys. They may not compare like with like. The same survey ranked the United States third. So, here you have one of the smallest countries as No.

---

[1] See Global City, Wikipedia. <http://en.wikipedia.org/wiki/Global_city>.

1, and one of the largest as No. 3. This is one reason why such surveys should be taken with a grain of salt.

Singapore is both a city and a nation-state. This complicates matters. Most foreigners think of Singapore simply as a city. But most Singaporeans think of Singapore in national terms. The government's stand lies in between these two views, although in recent times the Singapore government appears to have placed far greater emphasis on Singapore as a global city — at least that is the perception. This, by default, has had the unintended side effect of causing some fissures in the national fabric. It is possible to be both a global city and a nation-state. But it could be argued that the global city project pursued by Singapore has come at a heavy price for the nation-building project.

To establish a critical mass in population, so as to create what is known as "buzz," Singapore's doors have been thrown wide open to foreign nationals. No other country in recent times has seen an influx of foreign nationals of a similar magnitude. This has put pressure on infrastructure, such as housing and transport. And, while foreign nationals in other countries are only allowed to fill job vacancies that locals cannot fill, they are allowed here to compete directly with Singaporeans for existing jobs. With all things being equal, businesses will hire the person at the lowest cost.

The Singapore "grapevine" is rife with stories about how employers hire foreign workers on a specific grade of employment pass issued by the immigration authorities, declaring the minimum salary level stipulated by the pass and then circumventing that minimum salary level by making "deductions" for training, under-time, uniform and other gear, and so on. For example, an "S" pass holder with a minimum salary requirement of S$1,800 (which was raised to S$2,000 in 2011) could be paid between only S$1,200 and S$1,400 after all the deductions.[2]

In a society with a relatively high cost of living, there is a segment of Singaporeans who are not able to make ends meet with such salary levels.

---

[2] Ng, Esther and S Ramesh (2007). EP, S pass salary thresholds to be raised, *Today*, 10 March 2011. And Sim, Melissa (2007). Work pass: More bosses caught cheating, 7 October 2007. <http://www.asiaone.com/Business/News/Office/Story/A1Story20071011-29453.html>

But the world is filled with hundreds of millions of highly skilled individuals who are prepared to do jobs with a pittance of a salary, including S$1,200. Significant numbers have already migrated to Singapore and have displaced some Singaporeans from existing jobs. To that extent, there are increasing numbers of Singaporeans who feel uncertain about their place in their own country.

MONACO OF THE EAST

Expanding the scope of the service sector in Singapore's economy has been one of the ways of building up its global city status. Two of the most visible manifestations of this in recent years are the decision to hold an annual Formula One (F1) Singapore Night Race, and the introduction of casinos, which the Singapore government calls "integrated resorts (IR)." (The IR did not exist before 2004, which was when the Singapore government came up with the concept of introducing of casinos as part of sprawling entertainment resorts that would include high-end shopping, eateries, museums, and the like.)

The introduction of the F1 race and casinos prompted descriptions of Singapore as the "Monaco of the East," a phrase coined by Minister Mentor Lee Kuan Yew in 2005.[3]

The actual Monaco is typically described as a playground for the fabulously wealthy and famous. One website provides this description of Monaco: "A favourite of European royalty, Arab sheikhs, and opulently wealthy Americans who dock their mobile playground yachts in the marina."[4] Those who have visited both of the casinos in Singapore are likely to agree that the Singapore version of Monaco appears to fall far short of such descriptions. Discounting patrons in the VIP rooms, casino visitors — up to 40% of whom are Singaporeans — who traipse through the two gaming halls in Singapore are largely people who are least able to afford splurging on gambling sprees. Research has shown that Singaporeans are possibly some of the most avid gamblers in the world.[5] As to why this is the

---

[3] Burton, Jack (2009). Secrets of Success, *Financial Times*, 27 March 2009.

[4] Monaco Casino Royale. < http://www.onlinecasinojoy.com/monaco-casino-royale.html>

[5] Arnold, Wayne (2006). International Business; The Nanny State Places a Bet, *The New York Times*, 23 May 2006.

case, one conclusion is that Singaporeans live in such a compact and competitive society, where the punishment for poverty is of such frightening proportions, that it rewards greed and skews many Singaporeans' values towards material gain.

Just as was the case with another slogan — "Renaissance City of Asia" — which had been coined in 1998 to denote Singapore as a vibrant artistic and cultural hub, the slogan "Monaco of the East" also seems fated for eventual obscurity. A global city has to be global in all its dimensions, not just in its economic and infrastructural characteristics. And it cannot be a derivative of other cities. It has to be unique in a number of ways, so as to give it a competitive edge internationally.

THE BET ON CASINOS

On the surface at least, Singapore's IRs give it a sheen of sophistication. In reality, however, the resorts are just like the resorts in Macau — which are completely dependent on their casinos. The high-end retail outlets at Marina Bay Sands, for example, are largely spurned by visitors to the IR, as a 2010 *Today* article reported.[6] It seems that visitors have money to gamble away at the gaming tables, but not the money to spend on luxury merchandise.

However, all that may be immaterial as the revenues and profits of both casinos during their first incomplete calendar year of operations in 2010 exceeded even the most optimistic projections, generating hundreds of millions of dollars in profits within a matter of months.

The casinos and other facilities offered at the IR's have also created many new jobs, even if a significant number may have gone to foreigners.[7]

Moreover, the resorts have also had a positive spill-over effect on the wider economy. The combination of entry levies on Singaporeans and permanent residents and taxes on gaming profits now form a new and important revenue stream for the government.

---

[6] Yng, Ng Jing and Chin, Neo Chai (2010). MBS retail scene not as hot as expected, *Today*, 17 December 2010.
[7] Singapore Casino Jobs and Gaming-Related Careers.
<http://www.worldcasinojobs.com/singapore>

While there is a general consensus that these facts constitute a successful dimension to the IR project, there is a disinclination to recognise that the negative social impact of the casinos may have exceeded even the most pessimistic expectations.

Throughout 2010, the Singapore government repeatedly said that it was too early to determine the casinos' social impact, even as figures showed that by the end of December 2010, around 300 families had secured family exclusion orders to exclude a family member from the casinos. For every such order, it is likely that there were prior unsuccessful applications when the family member in question resisted attempts to be placed under such orders.

The same rule-of-thumb would apply to the reports of gamblers who were engaged in theft to fuel their binges at the casino. In a breakfast talk on the social and economic impact of the casinos, which I gave in August 2010 to some 30 KPMG auditors and accountants, I urged them to refresh their skills in the specialised area of forensic auditing. This was because I expected cases of fraud and theft in the months ahead, committed by gamblers siphoning money from their employers in order to fuel their casino visits. From the experience of other jurisdictions, it can take years for such white-collar crimes to come to light.

One of the consequences of having a casino industry in Singapore, despite all of its positive economic benefits, is that it would entrench an underclass and lead to social divisions. These are already significant in Singapore, and could get worse. Given Singapore's small size and population density, these divisions tend to be perceptually magnified many times over.

A DIVERSIFIED ECONOMY

Widening social divisions have become evident even as Singapore's economy has become more diversified and resilient. The influx of immigrants has helped in that process of diversification. Building up the population base with added foreign talent also ensures that Singapore will have a springboard for seizing new economic opportunities when they arise.

The issue at hand, however, is whether there is a disproportionate reliance on a small segment of the local population — 20% to 25% — to generate the vast bulk of economic growth.[8] In such a situation, spectacular headline numbers of economic growth come across as purely statistical in nature to the vast majority of the population. They may be impacted only marginally, in the form of nominal salary increments and bonuses.

Of course, significant economic growth also leads to rising property prices. That might be very material in many other countries, where people can draw what is known as equity from their residential property. But this generally does not apply in Singapore because some 86% of residential property comprises public housing and the rules governing Housing and Development Board (HDB) flats are such that owners are not allowed to pledge their flats as collateral for loans.

An economic strategy which results in a substantial and widening social and income gap between the top one-quarter of the population and the bottom three-quarters can only be sustained for a period of time — but not over the long haul, and clearly not indefinitely. For democratic entities, in the long run, this strategy will have inevitable political repercussions.

OPINIONS AND PRACTICES IN A GLOBAL CITY

In a global city, the opinions of the native-born and the immigrant population are given equal weight. This is what makes for the success of a global city — the acceptance of any number of opinions, whatever their origin. Another thing that is essential to a global city is that it subscribes to best international practices. This means more transparency and accountability. Policies can still be made by a small number of individuals, but these policies have to be explained so as to avoid speculation and second-guessing.

However, when a global city is also a nation-state, a portion of the local population may be less tolerant about accepting the opinions of non-citizens when it comes to sensitive national issues. This is where a global city and nation-state come into contention.

---

[8] Those who live in public housing are provided various social and financial assistance. The government terms this as "targeted assistance." Those who live in private housing receive very little, if anything. The 2010 figure of HDB dwellers are 76.3% of all stock of residential housing, hence estimated figure of 20% to 25% of private housing dwellers. Section 1.9 on *Residential Dwellings of the Department of Statistics 2011 Yearbook.*
<http://www.singstat.gov.sg/pubn/reference/yos11/yos2011.pdf>

The Singapore press regularly features commentaries by foreign nationals either living in or visiting Singapore, who offer high praise for the country and its government. For those who may not understand why such praise comes across as contentious, the reason can be summed up in a single word — condescension.

However, not everyone thinks so. In fact, there are those who feel that the regular evidence in the national dailies of how much non-citizens seem to love Singapore provides reassurance and vindication. Here, a distinction can be drawn with the attitude in truly First World societies. For instance, American author Kenneth Pyle, in his book *Japan Rising*, wrote that more than 100 years ago "the Japanese had no time for Japanophiles and took no pleasure in the patronising compliments of foreign visitors... The British poet Sir Edwin Arnold on a visit to Japan in 1891 was rebuked by the Japanese when he lavished praise on their traditional aesthetics."[9]

The same theme recurs in many other First World countries. For instance, a web posting on American culture for foreigners states: "The average American will not take kindly to bullying, condescension, line-jumping, or downright pushiness."[10]

The contention between the imperatives of being a nation-state and a global city will continue to play out in Singapore. At the time of writing (March 2011), Singapore was gearing up for a general election, whose results would provide an indication of where voter sentiments lie on this major issue. The 2011 election will be the most crucial in a generation. Its results will either give renewed vigour to Singapore's global city project, or it will decelerate that process.

---

[9] Pyle, Kenneth (2007). *Japan Rising*, New York: Public Affairs, p. 103.
[10] American Culture for Foreigners. < http://www.essortment.com/american-culture-foreigners-63697.html>

CHAPTER 2

Singapore as a Global City: A Balancing Act

SYLVIA LIM

One of the "Key Goals" recommended by the Economic Strategies Committee (ESC) Report 2010 is to further Singapore's position as a "Global City."

This goal was articulated to mean Singapore should be "vibrant and distinctive," "open and diverse," and "a home that provides an outstanding quality of life for our people" (Shanmugaratnam *et al.*, 2010).

While there is no doubt that Singapore needs to be plugged into the world outside its borders, it is submitted that Singapore faces certain inherent limitations in its quest to become a hub for creativity and innovation. These limitations must be addressed if it is to realise its full potential.

For example, Singapore is often seen as a sterile cultural desert with inadequate cultural activities to attract workers who are talented and highly skilled (Ooi, 2008). It is further submitted that enhancing Singapore's appeal as "home" must go beyond infrastructural spectacles and requires concrete measures to give Singaporeans a sense of empowerment and of being cared for within its porous borders.

HOW FAR CAN SINGAPORE BE A HUB FOR CREATIVITY AND INNOVATION IF IT MAINTAINS AN ILLIBERAL CLIMATE?

In its ranking of liveable cities in 2010, the Economist Intelligence Unit placed Singapore 53rd out of 140 cities (*The Straits Times*, 13 February

2010). Singapore's ranking was pulled down partly because of a low score for culture and environment.

This assessment exposes some challenges facing efforts to develop Singapore as an arts and creative capital, where "talented people....see this as a place where they can develop skills, expertise and creative imagination, achieve their aspirations, and contribute meaningfully to a society that is on the move," as advocated by the ESC Report.

Creativity typically thrives in free environments, which foster spontaneity, encourage the exploration of unconventional thought, encourage challenges to the status quo, and provide safety nets for failure. One dictionary meaning of "create" is to "bring into being out of nothing or by force of imagination." The micro-management of Singaporeans' everyday lives may not be the most conducive environment to nurture creativity and innovation.

As far as free expression is concerned, Singapore is not the most liberal of regimes. While the government may welcome commercial creativity and artistic activities that bring commercial benefits, it has been wary of activities which challenge the official social discourse.

Censorship is still a reality. Even a collaboration between Singaporeans and foreigners for Singaporeans to sing about their pet peeves as a "Complaints Choir" encountered problems when applying for a performing licence (Hansard, 15 February 2008). If this situation does not change, can Singapore ever claim to be an arts capital?

As for innovation in the commercial sector, there has been much government investment and many incentives to encourage research and development. Our potential in this area was addressed in the first Singapore Competitiveness Report in 2009 (Ketels, 2009). While noting Singapore's strong infrastructure, concerns were raised by industry players that the controlled nature of Singaporean society might inhibit "creative" activities that tend to thrive in less-structured environments.

Reasons why Singapore society has developed this way include decades of emphasis on "practical" knowledge in the education system and pragmatism as part of the work ethic. By and large, parents tend to encourage their children to take on "safe" jobs with established companies, rather than go into the creative industries or entrepreneurship. In addition, jobs in the elite administrative service are sought after as a fast route to success. A resident in his 30s, now successful in marketing, recently shared with the author that he did poorly in school as he was often faulted for being a "dreamer," which goes against the ethos of pragmatism preached by the state.

Why is the level of entrepreneurship in Singapore lower compared to many other countries? Some of the contributing factors, in my view, are an education system and culture that reward conformity and obedience, the fear of failure and the drastic consequences of failure. Being an undischarged bankrupt in Singapore, for instance, carries many disabilities and may not be worth the risk to many potential entrepreneurs.

One notable concern of the government is that talented people, including Singaporeans living overseas, must see Singapore as a place where they can make meaningful contributions. Indeed, the articulated aims of Singapore as a global city include making it a centre for leadership and ideas. People may have different ideas about how to contribute meaningfully, which may include becoming a pressure point for the government. Is the government prepared to embrace that?

THERE HAS BEEN A PALPABLE SENSE OF LOSS OF IDENTITY AND NATION IN VIEW OF THE RAPID PACE OF CHANGE IN THE LAST FEW YEARS

Although "Global City" and "Endearing Home" were articulated as twin aims in the government agenda, the writer's view is that there is an inherent contradiction between the two.

A simplistic illustration is Singapore's hosting of major meetings such as the International Monetary Fund and World Bank meetings in 2006. The tagline used then was the "Land of Four Million Smiles," which presumably intended to get the whole population smiling at the visitors.

However, due to the high security and traffic diversions, many people were inconvenienced and avoided the meeting area like plague, causing retailers in Suntec City to suffer significant business losses. It is doubtful that many locals were smiling during these meetings!

The concept of "Home" is an emotional one, which has nothing to do with more museums, new civic centres or being open to the world. Instead, the ordinary understanding of "Home" connotes familiarity and a sense of belonging.

An influx of foreigners over the last few years has resulted in a palpable sense of loss of identity and nationhood among Singaporeans.

There has been a drastic increase in the size of the population, from three million in 1990, to four million in 2000, and five million in 2010. Those who feel uncomfortable about this should note that the government has announced that it is using a population size of six and a half million as a planning parameter. These numbers, in an island of 700 square kilometres, are unimaginable to most of us.

Besides population density, the citizen to non-citizen mix has also changed. In 1990, 86% of the population comprised Singapore citizens. By 2010, this had fallen to 63%. This means that nearly four in ten here are non-citizens. This displacement affects the whole country, as Singapore has no hinterland. Unlike the residents of major cities like London or New York, locals here cannot move out of the city in order to seek refuge. Even in "heartland" areas like Tampines, one can close one's eyes at a traffic junction, listen to the surrounding conversations and imagine oneself to be in another country. Many Singaporeans feel that Singapore is "not recognisable anymore" and they are strangers in their own country.

The reaction from "the ground" has, naturally, not been good. Every day, the strains on infrastructure such as transport systems and other public amenities are keenly felt. During a recent personal encounter, a Singaporean told the writer that he disagreed with the government's exhortations to see foreigners as a form of healthy competition. In his view, the competition had reached unhealthy levels and is adversely affecting Singaporeans' quality of life.

In the face of these developments, how can Singaporeans feel more assured that they belong to Singapore rather than some other place? It is submitted that two important factors to address are empowering Singaporeans and showing them more care in our policies.

WE CAN RECLAIM SOME IDENTITY AND SOCIAL COHESION THROUGH EMPOWERMENT AND MUTUAL SUPPORT

Singaporeans must feel empowered at home.

To this end, it is felt that the government should retreat from spheres of life that are not central to government functions, and allow authentic leadership to grow organically. Examples of such spheres include sports associations, consumer groups and grassroots organisations. By facilitating the evolution of natural leaders, Singaporeans can "own" their pet causes and feel that they have a stake in Singapore's evolving society.

Political diversity should also be celebrated as an important means of keeping Singaporeans engaged in the country's direction and future. Not valuing such diversity creates the risk of apathy and cynicism towards "top-down" initiatives. Empowerment at home must include having diverse voices competing for public opinion, so that the public will be engaged in making choices that determine the country's directions.

Indeed, in the context of influx of foreigners into this country, the importance of the General Election as a reinforcement of the essence of Singapore citizenship cannot be under-estimated (Ting, 2010).

As for policies, it is time for Singaporeans to feel that they have intrinsic value and that the country will not fail them, especially when they are frail or old.

Hitherto, the official discourse has characterised welfare as a dirty word. Yet, Singapore is becoming an increasingly polarised society, with a widening income and wealth gap. Instead of embracing the future, many people find life worrying due to rising costs and issues facing the elderly.

The government policies regarding social protections are generally predicated on the principles of self-reliance and family support. How fair is this in practice?

The whole debate concerning the Central Provident Fund (CPF) Life initiative in 2007 was instructive. Reforms were made to the existing mandatory savings scheme, the CPF, to ensure that Singaporeans purchased annuities to provide monthly payments for life. This reform illustrated the government's worry that citizens would seek public financial assistance in their old age. Despite its strong financial position, the government would not countenance any suggestion of setting aside some funds in order to grow income to support seniors in their 80s (Hansard, 18 September 2007).

Medical costs are another area of concern. It is typical to come across sick senior citizens who are denied permission to draw on their compulsory medical savings accounts (Medisave) for various treatments, and who are instead forced to ask for money from their children to pay for medical bills.

A case in point is an elderly gentleman with a chronic illness, whom the author met recently. He had to regularly ask his son for cash for outpatient treatments, as his bills did not meet the Medisave withdrawal requirements. After his son got married and had a child, the son was saddled with his own family's medical bills, as well as other expenses. He then asked his father to move out to live with another child who, presumably, would take over the cash payments. Such tensions do not affect the wealthy, but rather the working and sandwiched classes. By requiring the elderly to exhaust their family resources, is this not tantamount to pass the buck to future generations, which the government has always warned against?

Each year, around 5,000 Singaporeans apply to the police for the Certificate of No Criminal Conviction, with 68% using it for permanent residency applications in other countries (Hansard, 25 August and 20 October 2008). It was reported in the press recently that some Singaporeans choose to immigrate to other countries because these had better social services. If Singaporeans are indeed immigrating to other countries because they believe other governments will take better care of them as permanent residents, it is high time to examine closely how well Singapore is caring for its own citizens.

REFERENCES

Ooi, Can–Seng (2008). *Credibility of a Creative Image: The Singaporean Approach*, Creative Encounters Working papers # 7, Copenhagen Business School.

Ketels, Christian *et al.* (2009). *Singapore Competitiveness Report*. Singapore: Asia Competitiveness Institute, Lee Kuan Yew School of Public Policy.

Hansard. Singapore Parliamentary Reports. Available online at http://www.parliament.gov.sg, accessed 13 January 2011.

Shanmugaratnam, Tharman. *et al* (2010). Economic Strategies Committee Report. Singapore. Available online at http://www.ecdl.org/media/Singapore%20Economic%20Committe 2010.pdf, accessed 5 December 2010.

Ting, Ming Hwa (2010). Ritual and identity: elections and voting in Singapore. *Taiwan Journal of Democracy* Vol 6, No. 2, pp. 101–124 (Dec 2010).

CHAPTER 3

I ...Singaporean

T. SASITHARAN

For everything that lives is holy, life delights in life...
Can I see another's woe, and not be in sorrow too?
Can I see another's grief, and not seek for kind relief?
—*William Blake*

The government has been prepossessed with the notion of turning Singapore into a global city for quite a while now. Our new "becoming," as it were, is clearly a national development priority. So much so, in fact, that becoming a global city has turned into something of a national obsession. In a city-state that is so meticulously structured and centrally managed, where some believe even the road-side trees are numbered and the presence of the government is both pervasive and persuasive, it is perhaps inevitable that we should be so obsessed. You see, nothing ensures obsequiousness in people like good old-fashioned national obsessions.

There is an inexorable logic to the selection of the model upon which Singapore's economic growth and national developments are predicated. Our economy is modelled after a particularly virulent strain of capitalism — a form of über-capitalism that is far more reliant on consumerism and materialism — a rabid proclivity to spend — than garden-variety capitalism. For it is only with the frenetic pace of über-capitalism that the government has any hope of sustaining the stratospheric rates of economic growth necessary to placate the people's material appetites and secure its own position, power and dominance in Singapore.

And so it begins: The unholy, interminable race to scramble up the constantly extending, slippery, value-chain of instrumentalist economics.

This endless scrambling upwards — always orderly, but, nonetheless, unseemly — has been the stuff of Singaporean life, indelibly imprinted in our collective subconscious, since our births and the birth of the Republic in 1965.

As so often happens in these circumstances, as with so many other government-inspired obsessions in Singapore, the prize of becoming a global city has now become something of a national fetish.

We are all familiar with this transmutation. An elective economic model, something that ought to be a matter of our choice, is seized upon by the state and turned into an absolute imperative, reducing, and ultimately condemning life in Singapore to the treadmill of teleology.

This is a uniquely Singaporean brand of nationalism — born of a dumb-struck populace, morally de-centred and rendered emotionally off-kilter through the incessant and tempestuous batterings of an all-consuming economy primed to perform at a feverish and, ultimately, impossible pitch.

As such, Singapore is in a state of perpetual prepossession; overcome, enervated by the withering absolute that is the economy. Stupid. Our lot as Singaporeans is one of perpetual anticipation and edginess, vulnerability and dis-ease. It is a feeling familiar to us all, a consequence of being in long, endless queues, all our lives.

Singaporean lives are, punctuated by acts of queuing — from pre-school in classrooms and canteens, to work-a-day lives in hawker-centres, The Mass Rapid Transit (MRT) stations and 4D counters. Our lives are measured by bouts of delirious anticipation.

We, the citizens of Singapore, pledge ourselves to wait quietly in line; in interminable lines, so as to cash in on the promissory note of a bigger, better, and brighter economy.

• • •

And so it has come to pass that becoming a global city has become our manifest destiny. It is now almost inevitable that we will become that brilliant, gleaming, pinnacle on the pile of the world's cities. What is more, if the rankings and the league tables and the surveys are to be believed, we are well on our way to being in the Alpha ++ league of cities.

This is, as such things tend to be here, almost, a fait accompli. Singapore is now, after all, the location of choice for such pinnacles of civilization and culture as the Sports Illustrated Swimsuit Edition (2011), The Martha Stewart Show and The Amazing Race. It appears, by any measure of significance to the government, that we have arrived.

But what does it really mean to be a global city? Surely it must mean more than vaulting towers and palaces, more than worldly power and influence and more than wealth and mere material gain. More surely, than being the undisputed location of choice for the next Bollywood or Hollywood blockbuster or F1 Grand Prix?

If we, as Singaporeans, must aspire to belong to a global city, then to aspire at all, at this particular juncture of human history, must mean more than merely aspiring to be a good city. It must mean that we must aspire to greatness — to be a great city.

Perhaps a Persepolis, Rome, Karakorum, London, Berlin, and New York, What do all those great cities have in common? They offered their populations — in their own shapes, ways, and forms — the possibility of transcendence. They engendered the means for their people to get above and beyond the vexatious flux of both the immediate and the material.

A truly great global city must be the site where the prerogatives and the encumbrances — the rights and the responsibilities — of citizenship to that city are conceived, contested, and eventually congealed. It must be the location where the identity of the citizen is formed and solidified; where the disparate and plural aspects of the personality and the self are fused and ordered; and where the fragments of the individual, private self that defy such an assay may, conclusively, be subordinated to the common, public identity that is entailed by the notion of "citizenship."

This, indeed, is the alchemy of national consensus, the transformation that a truly global city, a truly great city, enables in its citizens. This is the ultimate gift of the global city to its people.

It follows, therefore, that a true global city must possess a highly refined and acute sense of genius loci — spirit of place. Put another way, a great city must necessarily be a site where the souls of its citizens are forged; "soul" that is qua ontology, as an existential category of the self, rather than qua theology — that is, implying or concerning the Deity.

The bond between the city and its citizens is radically umbilical. Therein lies the root of the "rootedness" that moors the self to a place, and why so many people yearn to belong to a particular city. It is precisely because the bond is so radical that there is identification with a specific place. The radicality of this identification is the basis and bedrock of the claim that a particular city is "my home."

This bond, its radicality, and the identification that it engenders are why some people will give their lives for their cities. As history has proven time and again, people will die to protect their homes.

The desire for this bonding is sometimes so urgent and so palpable that it manifests as pure aspiration. Consider its invocation by United States president John F. Kennedy on 26 June 1963. At the height of the Cold War, he said in Berlin:

> Two thousand years ago the proudest boast was
> Civis Romanus Sum. Today, in the world of freedom,
> the proudest boast is Ich bin ein Berliner.

The need for such bonding can be so intense and so overwhelming that it might be asserted or assumed even when citizenship is explicitly denied and only subjecthood is proffered. See, for example, Nirad C. Chaudhuri's dedication for his novel *The Autobiography of an Unknown Indian* (1951):

> To the memory of the British Empire in India,

> Which conferred subjecthood upon us,
> But withheld citizenship.
> To which yet every one of us threw out the challenge:

> "Civis Britannicus Sum"

> Because all that was good and living within us
> Was made, shaped and quickened
> By the same British rule.

• • •

In unpacking the meaning of Singapore for Singaporeans, in terms of the notions of home, of our deep need and desire to belong to and identify with a city — "because all that [is] good and living within us/ was made, shaped, and quickened [here]" — we discover, remarkably, a bond that is more uniquely binding, more compact, more intense, and more forceful, compared to equivalent relationships between other cities and their citizens.

The uniqueness of being Singaporean arises not because Singapore is culturally or historically exceptional, but because of Singapore's preposterously small size. It comes down to our geography.

You see, in Singapore's case, in our case, our city is all that is the case. There is nothing more — no larger hinterland to speak of, no difference between urban and rural, no bigger country or countryside. No ameliorations of geography, either physical or mental, are available to us.

There is no calibrating frame of reference or comforting context afforded by territoriality. There are no other enabling circumstances or conditions of materiality; no significant temporal distance or separation wherein our city may be conceived or imagined or enacted; swathed, contained, lighted in space and time as scene and setting.

There simply is no theatre wherein to play out the performance of Singapore's nationhood. Singapore is all there is for us; at once, city-state-nation. It is all, for Singaporeans.

This apparent wholeness is, without a doubt, a remarkable confabulation. And there is a brutal inescapability about its improbable morphology. Singapore's existence, its very being, is about as far removed from any notion of the "natural" as it is possible to imagine; it is a purely willed whole, an artifice of determination.

This, of course, is completely at odds with the usual state of these things, the way states are "supposed to be." Singapore is, in fact, positively "unnatural."

More than two centuries of slow, deliberate, and directed progress separates the conception of the sovereign state, with its permanent borders and territories (read Treaty of Westphalia,1648), from the only idea of nationhood which is singularly relevant to us today as Singaporeans.

The only idea of nationhood relevant to the Singapore of today, which aspires to be a great global city, is this one: The notion of nationhood as a moral and existential formation, a "spiritual principle" centred in a "soul." This idea of nationhood was articulated by Ernest Renan (*What is a Nation?* 1882):

A nation is a soul, a spiritual principle. Two things, which in truth are but one, constitute this soul or spiritual principle. One lies in the past, one in the present. One is the possession in common of a rich legacy of memories; the other is the present-day consent, the desire to live together, the will to perpetuate the value of the heritage that one has received in an undivided form.

A nation is therefore a large-scale solidarity, constituted by the feeling of the sacrifices that one has made in the past and of those that one is prepared to make in the future. It presupposes a past; it is summarized, however, in the present by a tangible fact, namely, consent, the clearly expressed desire to continue a common life..

Man is a slave neither of his race nor his language, nor of his religion, nor of the course of rivers nor the direction taken by mountain chains. A large aggregate of men, healthy in mind and warm of heart, creates the kind of moral conscience which we call a nation. So long as this moral consciousness gives proof of its strength by the sacrifices which demand the abdication of the individual to the advantage of the community, it is legitimate and has the right to exist. [my emphasis]

In Europe, the process of conjoining the notion of the sovereign state with that of the nation was torn to shreds and nearly destroyed beyond repair by two catastrophic world wars over 50 years. It bears pointing out that any claim to legitimacy Singapore might have as a sovereign state is less than 50 years old, and any notions that Singaporeans may harbour of being a nation is at least as long a time away — in a mist-filled, optimistic future. The process of Singapore's "ensouling," of forming a soul, however, has already begun in earnest; of that, there is absolutely no doubt.

We are neither a large aggregate nor a large solidarity. We have no rich common heritage; any richness of heritage we might possess is born of deep differences and diversity and plurality, the very antitheses of commonality.

But we do possess a legacy of memories of a past compactly lived; feelings of pride and strength born of ordinary, everyday sufferings and sacrifices that Singaporeans of every ilk, creed, colour and class made, and continue to make, in the continuous struggle to get by.

This struggle to be — the simple, unadorned act of getting by — has been played out a million times, enacted by countless folk over the last 50 years. This is the signification of our consent for a continued common life. Our lives are the vessels of our "expressed desire" and our sacrifice of the personal and the individual for the good of the whole and the weal of the commons.

It is precisely in the everyday struggle of the people to be, the quotidian "health of mind" and "warmth of heart," the ceaseless faith and industry of the ordinary Singaporean, that our collective moral conscience lives.

This is the aforesaid "ensouling" — the incipient quickening of the moral and spiritual principle mingled with a lived experience, which will, in the fullness of time, become our soul. This is all it is: An existential essence, life; our lives, lived at once individually and collectively.

This is the very thing-process that the Irishman James Joyce so beautifully celebrated in his novel *A Portrait of the Artist as a Young Man*:

> Welcome, O life!
> I go to encounter for the millionth time the reality of
> experience and to forge in the smithy of my soul the
> uncreated conscience of my race.

Singaporean lives, our encounter with the reality of experience, could bear a far better telling than they have been accorded thus far.

The people of Singapore deserve an honest telling, one that is as far removed from being propaganda or advertising as is humanly and creatively possible. Singaporeans deserve a beautiful telling, guided by our incipient moral sensibility and by the reality of life. We deserve this rather than what we currently have — ugly, unwieldy narratives tainted by the provisional pettiness and the partisanship of political processes skewed by the overweening presence of a single, puffed-up, tiresomely dominant political party.

Singaporeans deserve better. This is a truth both our government and our citizens (the artists, in particular) should heed in equal measure.

• • •

On 25 September 2009, the last day of the International Federation of Arts Councils and Culture Agencies' (IFACCA) fourth World Summit on Arts and Culture in Johannesburg, South Africa, I had the singular pleasure of meeting Justice Albie Sachs, a judge of the Constitutional Court of South Africa. He was appointed to the court by Nelson Mandela himself.

Justice Sachs, who opposed apartheid, had lost his right arm and an eye to a bomb placed in his car in 1988 by South African state security agents. He is, clearly, a man who knows a thing or two about what it means to struggle for freedom and justice; about fighting for the oppressed and dying for one's home; about the soul of men and of nations.

"Hello," I said, extending my left hand. "I am from Singapore." He took my hand, smiled, fixed me with his one good eye, and said, "Ah! you have everything except a soul."

He might as well have slapped me in the face or kicked me in the gut. I was winded; but managed a grimaced smile before the hurt flooded through me. Why was I hurt? Because this exceptional man was spot-on in his assessment of us, as Singaporeans. By every estimation, we do have everything. And yet, by some honest estimation, we are soulless.

I wish I had told him then that some Singaporeans know that their country lacks a soul. But they also know full well that the souls of nations are forged through great labour, and with great faith and great sacrifice. And that we, as a people, in the millions of moments of our shared lives and in myriad uncountable ways, have already started on the long trek of building a soul for our beloved country.

One day, we, too, will gain the voice to speak truth to power. We will stand up as a people, in the defense of the freedoms of all fellow Singaporeans — men and women — bear witness to and break down the illegitimate controls of the state on people's legitimate rights of protest, dissent, and assembly. We will defend free speech and expression, and speak on behalf of the powerless, the poor, the oppressed, and the weak.

On that day, we will be able to openly acknowledge those who had walked ahead of us — people like Joshua Benjamin Jeyaretnam, Kuo Pao Kun, Chia Thye Poh, Lim Hock Siew, Vincent Cheng, Teo Soh Lung, and many others, who had the courage of their convictions and suffered bitterly for it. By having such courage, they served and sacrificed more than most in the shaping of Singapore's soul.

We may not all of us live to see that day. But I am certain our children will, and that will do just fine.

DISCUSSANT NOTES

ONG YE KUNG
Panel on Global City

As a discussant, and in keeping with the spirit of the Conference, my role is to provide an alternative perspective on the issues raised by the panelists.

My key takeaway from the presentation by Mr Derek Da Cunha was his observation that the Integrated Resorts (IRs) have created significant social problems, in terms of "problem gambling." This was a key consideration when the Government was deciding whether to proceed with the IRs.

Notwithstanding, we should also recognise the many positive benefits of the IRs. The IRs collectively and directly created 20,000 jobs, and indirectly generated tens of thousands of other jobs. I once had an encounter with a croupier who managed to double her pay compared to her previous job, which changed her life. I also met another graduate who was happily working as an attraction host in Universal Studio, and was likely to participate in a management associate programme in Resorts World Sentosa. Moving forward, we needed to ensure we reap the benefits, but minimise the social fall-out of the IRs.

The IRs have also set a new benchmark for jobs in the service sector, and have led to non-IR hotels and attractions raising their training standards and employment terms. This was one key reason why Singapore continued to create jobs during the Global Financial Crisis in 2008.

There were two key takeaways from Ms Sylvia Lim's presentation. One was her call for greater empowerment of Singaporeans. My view is that a big part of empowerment for Singaporeans, particularly for young Singaporeans, is to provide them with a good education and skills training, connections to the world and opportunities to fulfill their dreams and hopes. I am very cheered by the dynamism and creativity of youths today, amply displayed in our schools, and during major national events, when youths come forward to volunteer their services.

The second key takeaway was Ms Lim's concern that globalisation and greater immigration has diluted the Singaporean identity. I feel that globalisation has become an inescapable reality, which every country in the world grapples with. Policies have to be calibrated over time, which is why the Government recently tightened the inflow of foreign workers.

It would serve us better to make the best use of globalisation to strengthen our national and cultural identity, rather than bemoan its negative impact. Globalisation is similar to the Internet, which can be put to both good and bad uses, and we must look at the positive side of this inevitable phenomenon.

For example, with a global communications network, we can better engage overseas Singaporeans and strengthen their sense of national identity. Our companies are venturing overseas, exporting the Singaporean way of doing things abroad. The Marina Bay skyline is a product of globalisation, and has become a globally recognisable landmark. As a Singaporean, I am proud of it, and believe that over time it will become another icon that Singaporeans find endearing.

The key takeaway from Mr Sasitharan's presentation was the concern that Singaporeans lack soul. I hold a different view. Singapore does not have the history of China, India, Europe, and many other nations, and so we cannot expect our young nation to even approximate the cultural depths of these countries.

But within a generation, we have achieved many unthinkable feats — progressing from Third World to First, becoming self-sufficient in water, building up world-class seaports and airports, housing the great majority of our population, hosting the inaugural Youth Olympics, among other achievements. All these have showed that we are a people with determination and character, and this provides a very strong basis upon which to build our nation and nurture our soul.

III

Caring Community

Singapore's economic success has been both bane and boon. Contributions by the citizens have formed the bedrock of the country's stunning progress and transformation. As Singapore enters a new era of development shaped by internal and external changes, it is timely to re-examine and if necessary, to refine ways in which Singaporeans can provide better care for their fellow citizens. In particular, the population is ageing fast and those with special needs require more state attention. The expectations of Singaporeans are also changing as the demography of the population transforms. How can we grow together while maintaining social mobility? How can we ensure that each citizen has a share in Singapore's growth? How can we express care and concern for our fellow citizens in a more responsive and effective fashion? Is minimum wage the solution to increasingly unbalanced income distribution? While state and grassroots organisations have been providing services under the "Many Helping Hands" approach, individual involvement and engagement is invaluable. Is there a way to ensure the increased effectiveness of customised care? A cohesive Singapore requires strong personal commitment and participation. Are Singaporeans capable of more philanthropic and volunteer work?

CHAPTER 4

We Do Care....or Do We?

T. RAJA SEGAR

When I was asked to present a paper on the theme "Caring Community," two titles popped into my head: "We do care....or do we?" and "Caring from a distance."

My scepticism stems from my experiences since joining the Singapore Indian Development Association (SINDA) two and a half years ago. Part Voluntary Welfare Organisation (VWO), part social service organisation and part institution for students from low-income families, almost 70% of SINDA's budget depends on donations.

We do have a large pool of volunteers, but the type of volunteers we attract has been changing over the years. There are more ad-hoc or occasional volunteers now when compared to a decade ago. One can only hazard a guess as to why this change has come about. It could be due to the changing lifestyle of Singaporeans. Employees from both the public and the private sectors now tend to travel more for work. Setting aside time for a continuous period has become increasingly difficult.

Parents are more engaged with their families and their leisure time is reserved for that purpose. We also have more options during our free time. We are spending more time on the Internet. We spend time on entertainment, shopping, eating, etc. Volunteers are willing to commit short spurts of their time — this is now a more feasible option for them.

When this paper was presented, large parts of the state of Queensland in Australia were experiencing one of the worst floods of the past century. While most Queenslanders were affected in some way, many came forward to help those in need while nursing their own tragedies. I felt that this spontaneous volunteerism illustrated a genuine outpouring of care and concern. I questioned if Singaporeans would have displayed that same spontaneity if a disaster had struck Singapore, or whether we would have waited for the relevant authorities to act and played second fiddle ourselves — acting only if required and instructed to do so. I feel that there is a strong "someone else will take care of it" attitude among Singaporeans.

Care is an important component of a civil society. Human beings are comforted by the fact that we are cared for in our different social contexts. This is a psychological need. We belong to a family, a group of friends, a school, a company; we often associate ourselves with groups to ensure that we are not left out. I believe that this need to be cared for is felt by all, particularly by those who are not doing well in life. For the residents of a nation to progress together, it is important that we develop a sense of care for everyone. We need to be able to measure this via relevant proxies, in order to keep tabs on whether we are indeed progressing in this respect or slipping.

What constitutes an appropriate "Care Index"? The closest proxies in my mind are the donor and volunteer statistics of a country. For Singapore, these statistics are captured in the Individual Giving Survey conducted annually by the National Volunteer and Philanthropy Centre (NVPC). In my paper, I have used the survey results published in September 2008 and November 2010.

The NVPC study shows that Singaporeans would rather donate money than spend time helping other Singaporeans in need. Singaporeans score high as donors but low on volunteerism. While donations are essential for the running of any social service organisation, dedicated volunteers make all the difference in the lives of the people who need care and concern more than anything else.

Thus, we can say that we are getting mixed signals in Singapore. Singaporeans are generous donors and respond well to appeals. For a tiny country, we donate comparatively generously when responding to disasters. When the world went into recession and Singapore had its fair share of woes, most social service organisations budgeted for significant deficits. This was not only because they wanted to spend more to cushion the impact of the recession for their constituents, but also because they thought that donors would be hard-pressed to continue donating as much as they had during the good years.

But most of these organisations were pleasantly surprised about the final tally of donations that poured in. Singaporean individuals and corporations came forth with alacrity to support the social service sector with donations that more or less took care of their increased expenditures, or at least reduced their actual deficits versus planned deficits. While some might dismiss this as a response to tax exemption schemes for Institutions of Public Character (IPCs) announced by the government, I believe that a genuine sense of wanting to help those in need — perhaps while also benefiting from the tax exemption schemes — lies at the heart of the matter.

DONATION STATISTICS

The Individual Giving Survey 2010 by NVPC states that Singapore is ahead of the United Kingdom and the United States in terms of percentage of individuals who had donated in the last 12 months (See Figure 1). The survey shows that in 2010, we crossed the $1 billion mark for donations by individuals. This is a very credible figure given that we are a nation of about five million, with about three million represented in the labour force. There are concerted efforts across all platforms — such as schools, offices, places of worship, and commercial outlets — to solicit for donations when we are faced with a situation that warrants more funds. Whether it is an earthquake in India or China, or a tsunami in Indonesia or Japan, we tend to show our support in a significant manner.

However, I believe that the right indicator for care is not the amount of donations received, but rather the level or amount of direct work done with those who need our assistance. Thus, volunteer numbers and hours spent on voluntary welfare or community work may be a better estimate of how much we really do care as a society.

This paradox is aptly illustrated in the following graphs from the "Individual Giving Survey 2010."

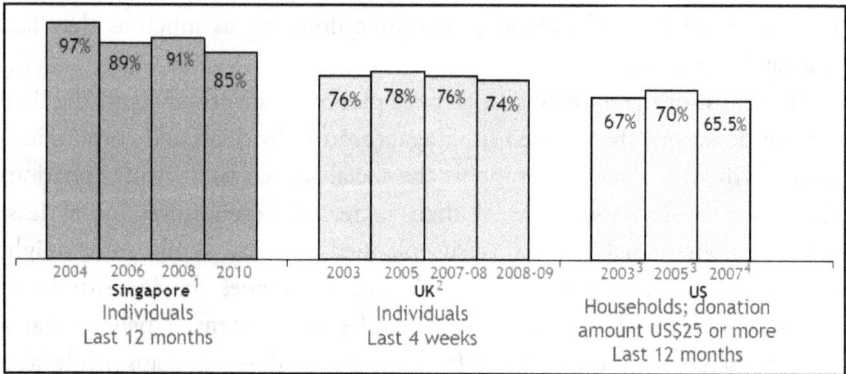

Figure 1 Singapore led in giving money

Sources:

1 Individual Giving Survey (2004, 2006, 2008, 2010), National Volunteer and Philanthropy Centre, Singapore.

2 2008-09 Citizenship Survey: Volunteering and Charitable Giving Topic Report (2010), Department for Communities and Local Government, United Kingdom. Retrieved 27 September 2010 from <http://www.communities.gov.uk/documents/statistics/pdf/1547056.pdf>. UK information previously reported in IGS2008 results was from a different source: Helping Out(2007), Cabinet Office, United Kingdom.

3 Center on Philanthropy Panel Study. (2003, 2005), The Center on Philanthropy at Indiana University, United States.

4 Overview of Overall Giving: Based on data collected in 2007 about giving in 2006 (2010), The Center on Philanthropy at Indiana University, United States. Retrieved 28 September 2010 from <http://www.philanthropy.iupui.edu/research/copps/docs/2007COPPS_KeyFindin gs.pdf>.

The histogram comparing Singapore, the United States, and United Kingdom may not provide a good comparison since we are not aware of the base information and the questions asked. Furthermore, Singapore's structured donation schemes included flag days and monthly contributions to self-help groups, which may have influenced the results — 85% of the respondents stated that they had donated in the last 12 months. There may not be similar schemes in other countries. While donations are generally on a voluntary basis in most countries, the set-up of self-help groups on ethnic lines in Singapore is deemed as a pro-active step, to draw donors to fund community-led social and educational support programmes.

The survey also showed that almost 60% of donations were made to religious organisations. This, too, may have influenced the higher rate of donations in Singapore, where a significantly higher percentage of the population profess a religion, compared to the UK and the US. Most religions mandate or strongly encourage donations to religious establishments. Such donations are used to support the rituals of these religions, as well as the less fortunate among the congregation.

In dollar terms, Singaporeans donated more compared to previous years, although donor trends dropped in 2010 (refer to Figures 2 and 3). This could be attributed to the impact of the 2008 and 2009 recession on individuals, but those who continued to donate compensated by donating larger amounts. This probably points to the sense of empathy that many of the bigger donors feel for others in the community, or the probability that the business community donates more due to higher tax exemptions.

Figure 2 Donor incidence from 2004 to 2010

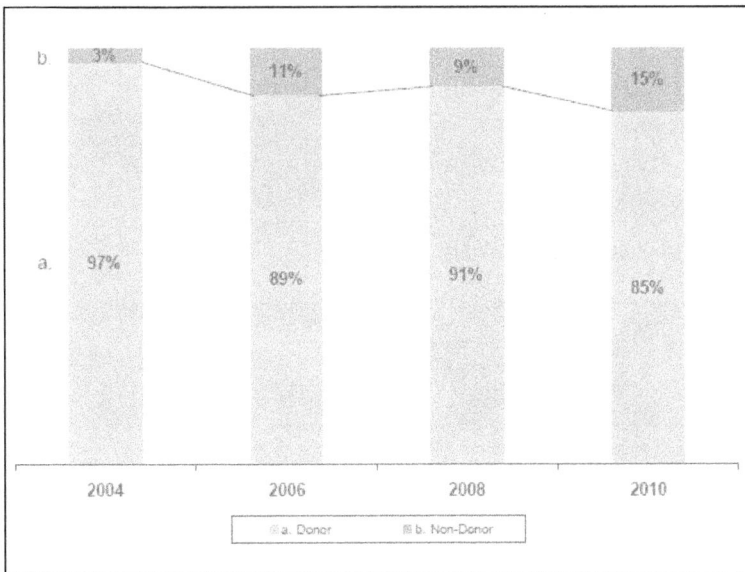

Source: Individual Giving Survey 2010, NVPC

Figure 3 Individual and total donations

Year	Average Donation	Total Giving of Money by Individuals
2004	S$155 per giver	S$438 million
2006	S$125 per giver	S$341 million
2008	S$300 per giver	S$958 million
2010	S$331 per giver	S$1,067 million

Source: Individual Giving Survey 2010, NVPC

VOLUNTEERISM

When it comes to volunteering, Singaporeans take a back seat. The survey found that 23.3% of the Singapore population were engaged in formal and informal volunteering. Though this was an improvement from the 15.2% recorded in 2004, the bigger question is: Is this enough? Even among the volunteers, about 55% are occasional volunteers, as opposed to volunteering regularly on a weekly or monthly basis. The percentage of weekly volunteers is about 22% and has not changed over the last five years (Refer to Figure 4). However, total volunteer hours have increased significantly. (Refer to Figure 5.)

Figure 4 Volunteer frequency

Volunteer Frequency	% of Current Volunteers		
	2006	2008	2010
Weekly (per week)	21%	24%	22%
Monthly (per month)	25%	22%	22%
Occasionally (per year)	54%	54%	55%

Source: Individual Giving Survey 2010, NVPC

Figure 5 Volunteer hours

Year	Incidence of Current Volunteers	Total Volunteer Hours (exclude travelling time)
2006	15.5%	49 million hours
2008	16.9%	45 million hours
2010	23.3%	89 million hours

Source: Individual Giving Survey 2010, NVPC

One thing that stands out is the fact that we have given less in terms of our time. This may be due to lack of time, or a changing mindset which presumes that monetary donations can replace volunteering our time for social causes.

Figure 6 Singapore lagged behind in giving time

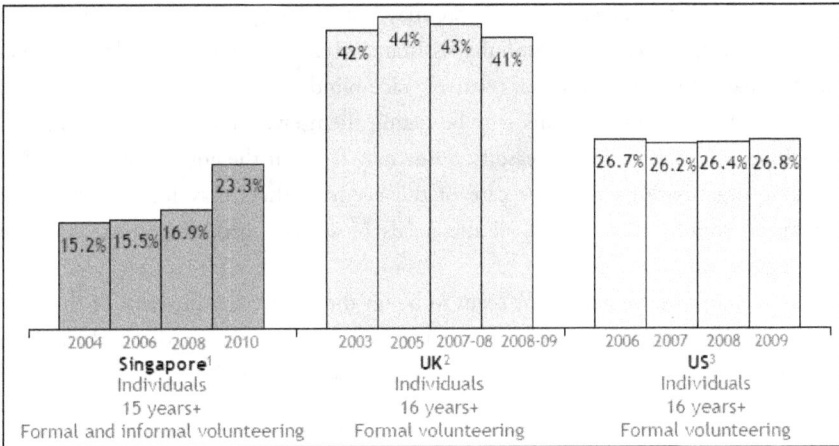

Source: Individual Giving Survey 2010, NVPC

The comparison between Figure 6 with Figure 1 sums up my argument that Singaporeans donate generously but are not willing to commit time. The above graph excludes the time spent by students doing community projects as part of their school activities.

CONCLUSION

Are Singaporeans truly cognizant of the needy among us? Does care overflow from "natural concern" among people in the community, or are structures (aims, vision, and key performance indicators) in schools and companies driving our behaviour? The Community Involvement Programme (CIP) is mandatory in some schools for graduation purposes. I note that the CIP programme requirements may allow students to experience the joy of volunteering at a young age, and would ideally spur them to become self-motivated volunteers when they are older. While I appreciate this system, I believe that encouraging volunteering through mandatory means may not be the most natural way of instilling the spirit of volunteerism in schoolchildren.

Another pertinent question to ask is whether we are colour-blind in terms of race when giving donations and volunteering for a cause. While Corporate Social Responsibility (CSR) activities led by companies tend to help any deserving VWO, self-help groups tend to draw volunteers and donations from the specific communities that they represent. There may not be conscious efforts to promote a multi-racial approach to community assistance, but corporate-led or large formal groups that lead social causes are relatively race-blind.

I believe that Singaporeans may be taking themselves out of the equation to a certain extent, due to several reasons. Some may feel that the government and other funding organisations will take care of the needy. Others may feel that their tax payments should take care of all the needs of society, including those who are lagging behind.

In conclusion, Singaporeans seem to be on the right track in terms of thinking about helping others. But they still need to be persuaded to contribute their time, and not restrict to donations alone. In this way, we will develop a nation of people who truly care for each other.

REFERENCES

1. *Individual Giving Survey 2010*, National Volunteer and Philanthropy Centre (NVPC), November 2010.
2. *Individual Giving Survey 2008*, National Volunteer and Philanthropy Centre (NVPC), September 2008.

CHAPTER 5

Including the Disadvantaged in a Meritocratic Singapore: Past, Present and Future

DENISE PHUA

INTRODUCTION

Good morning, your Excellencies, Ladies, and Gentlemen. Thank you for giving me the opportunity to share my perspective at this Technology Entertainment and Design (TED)-like platform.[1]

The path of forging a more inclusive Singapore society is one of no return. As expectations rise in an increasingly progressive and affluent Singapore, the voices of different interest groups will only grow louder.

When I shared on Facebook that I would be speaking at this seminar, a passionate animal rights advocate reminded me to lobby for the interests of animals and ensure that evil animal abusers, including any relevant government agencies, would be taken to task.

One only has to scan the Internet to hear the voices of many groups who seek inclusion, state's attention and resources. These include the low-income earners, the disabled, human rights activists, animal rights activists,

---

[1] Online talks by interesting people <http://www.ted.com/>

the elderly, same-sex couples, religious groups, atheists, performance artists, as well as political parties. There is also the notion of an "e-inclusive society," where everybody is able to reap the benefits brought about by information and communications technologies. Advocates for this ideology want technology to be accessible and affordable for all, regardless of age, language, social background or ability.

But *who* should be prioritized for inclusion and provision, in the face of finite time and resources, especially if each group feels they deserve priority? We may never agree on the answer. But most of us will agree that the real wealth of a nation is reflected not only by the size of its coffers, but also in the way it includes and cares for those who are vulnerable and disadvantaged. For what shall it profit a man, if he shall gain the whole world, and lose his own soul?

In the interest of time, I will focus primarily on two groups of vulnerable Singaporeans who are at risk of being left behind. They are those in the lower economic strata of Singapore, and the disabled - young and elderly. The State is constantly under pressure to cater for members of these groups, in order to prevent a serious loss of social bonding, disunity and instability.

ON ENABLING AND INCLUDING THE DISABLED

Since Prime Minister Lee Hsien Loong announced the vision to create a more inclusive society during his 2004 inauguration, there has been much progress, especially for people with special needs in Singapore. In 2007, the Government commissioned the drafting of a new five year Enabling Masterplan by key community leaders and boldly accepted almost all their recommendations. Even politicians from opposition parties admitted that "for many years, prior to the birth of (this) Enabling Masterplan, "disadvantaged" Singaporeans [were] virtually an invisible group of citizens in our society."[2]

Indeed, when it comes to including the disabled, significant progress had been made over the last five years. This progress is the result of a caring community comprising the Government and agencies such as the National

---

[2] The Excluded in an Inclusive Society, 31 January 2008, the Workers' Party website, <http://wp.sg/2008/01/the-excluded-in-an-inclusive-society/>

Council of Social Services (NCSS) and Voluntary Welfare Organisations (VWOs) that champion and advocate for inclusion and resources.

Some areas of progress include the following:

(a) The number of Early Intervention Programme for Infants and Children (EIPIC) centres increased from three in 2003 to 11 in 2010;

(b) Although Early Intervention, like most other social service programmes, is means-tested, a new fixed subsidy of $300 per citizen child was introduced, making the costly EIPIC programme far more affordable to all Singaporeans;

(c) A Special Needs Trust Company and a revamped Centre for Enabling Living to serve both the disabled and the elderly-in-need have been set up;

(d) The Ministry of Education, which formerly took an arms-length approach to the education of special-needs students, has stepped up very actively to improve the effectiveness and quality of special schools; and

(e) Efforts to include adults with disabilities and to ensure they have access to employment support and community integration are underway, although there is still a general dearth of these services.

There is still much to do in terms of raising the bar for essential services to the disabled community. This has hitherto been left to the care of the charity sector, but there is now a light at the end of the tunnel for those in need.

ON INCLUDING THE POOR AND LOW-SKILLED

As for the poor and low-wage, low-skilled population, last week's robust Parliamentary debate on inclusive growth has highlighted their plight and re-affirmed Singapore's conviction that they should not be left behind.

Whilst globalisation has fuelled Singapore's economic growth, not all have benefited equally from this growth. Singapore's highly educated and skilled workers are sought locally and overseas, leading to an inevitable hike in their income. On the other hand, many low-skilled workers, especially those in low-end production jobs, face the daily risk of losing their jobs to countries of lower cost.

Unless they upgrade their skills in time, they will become either permanently redundant or chronic low-wage workers, stuck in what I call the "3-L" (low pay, low status, and long hours) industries that cannot be relocated overseas. These are the cleaning, food and beverage, laundry and other service industries. Ensuring these low-skilled workers are not left behind in the wake of Singapore's economic growth is important.

Schemes such as the Workfare Income Supplement scheme anchors inclusive growth. Introduced in 2007, some 400,000 low-wage workers with gross monthly incomes of up to $1,700 per month saw a total top-up of $400 million to date. There is also the Workfare Training Support scheme and a national Workforce Skills Qualifications (WSQ) framework to certify skills and lay the pathways for Continued Education and Training. There are Productivity and Innovation Initiatives, the latest being the National Trades Union Congress (NTUC) Employment and Employability Institute's $40 million Inclusive Growth Programme. Other schemes include the restriction of foreign labour in order to encourage local hiring.

In addition, the poor in our country benefit from a slew of social assistance programmes if they qualify under means-testing. These include:

(a) Home Ownership and Upkeep, which includes the Rent and Utilities Assistance Scheme; Home Ownership Plus Education Scheme;

(b) Healthcare – Medisave, Medishield, Medifund;

(c) Education — Kindergarten Financial Assistance Scheme; Student Care Free Assistance Scheme Centre-based Financial Assistance Scheme for Child Care;

(d) Compulsory Savings such as the Central Provident Fund (CPF), Singapore's version of Social Security; and

(e) Transfers such as the Goods and Service Tax (GST) credits, utilities and rental rebates and public assistance for some 2,000 elderly citizens with no family support.

However, these measures are not always perfect. As the cost of living escalates, there is a need to constantly tweak the configuration of these help schemes to take care of those who are at risk of becoming chronic low-wage or even no-wage workers, due to their inability to learn or catch up. Suggestions to increase workfare, a government-paid income top-up scheme; increase the cash portion of the payout; and escalate efforts to transform low-productivity jobs have been tabled and are now under consideration.

I have also requested that the public sector identifies and awards contracts or jobs to workers who cannot benefit from further training due to their advanced age and/or lower learning abilities. Many of these workers are the last to be hired and first to be fired. I hope that my proposal is heeded.

PRINCIPLES UNDERPINNING SINGAPORE'S SOCIAL SAFETY NET

The three basic principles underlying the social safety net are:

(a) Self-reliance, or work before welfare
(b) Family as the first line of defence
(c) Many Helping Hands.

PRINCIPLE ONE: SELF-RELIANCE, WORK BEFORE WELFARE

The principle of self-reliance underlines the support schemes for Singapore's poor, which encourages individuals to work before seeking welfare. This is the path that is uniquely Singaporean, and one that is less travelled than the path of welfarism.

It is telling that this supplement is paid out in the form of work incentives to encourage work, rather than in the form of unemployment benefits for those with no work.

In the face of data that the average Singaporean can live into his or her 80s, measures have been put in place to encourage Singaporeans to be in the workforce for a longer period of time; to build a bigger nest egg; and to take up annuity schemes such as CPF Life, so as to enhance the financial security of the elderly. Active ageing programmes have also been put in place so that senior citizens can enjoy a good quality of life during their golden years.

The implementation of these measures is not without challenges:

(a) There is the constant appeal of the more universally applied Minimum Wage Policy versus the unique Singaporean Workfare Income Supplement scheme, where pay is topped-up by the Government;

(b) Even as Members of Parliament (MPs) urge the raising of the Workfare Income Supplement in order to top up the pay of low-wage workers, there is fear of whether this would reduce the motivation of these workers to train or upgrade their skills for a potential rise in income; and

(c) While research has shown that a significant number of Singaporeans are financially ill-prepared for retirement, many remain resistant to the raising of the retirement and CPF withdrawal age. "Stop treating me like a child. Give me my money. I will cross the bridge when it comes if I do not have sufficient resources to live on for the latter part of my life." Such are the tensions behind the principle of self-reliance. Alas, not everyone agrees with the principle of self-reliance except the likes of poet Ralph Waldo Emerson, who said this of self-reliance and the beauty of work: "There is a time in every man's education when he arrives at the conviction that envy is ignorance; that imitation is suicide; that he must take himself for better, for worse, as his portion; that though the wide universe is full of good, no kernel of nourishing corn can come to him but through his toil bestowed on that plot of ground which is given to him to till."

PRINCIPLE TWO: FAMILY — THE FIRST LINE OF DEFENCE

The second principle underlying Singapore's social safety net is that the family is the first port of call in times of difficulty, failing which the community and the Government will step in.

Family members are encouraged to care for one another, with the support of Government-initiated legislative and administrative measures:

(a) The CPF Minimum Sum Topping-Up Scheme, for instance, encourages children to voluntarily top up their parents' accounts. Tax relief is given for these top-ups;

(b) Tax incentive in the form of parent relief is also extended to Singaporeans who look after the elderly;

(c) One can use Medisave for the medical care of family members.

The Maintenance of Parents Act states the floor or minimum standard of parental care expected of an adult child and the consequences he will face if he disregards the call to feed and clothe his own parents when he is able to afford it. Recent amendments to the Act have created more space for conciliation before a formal submission of a claim, in order to preserve family relationships.

But what happens if the family does not want to be the first port of call in the event of difficulties? What happens when parties claim that issues such as providing for one's parents are personal choices and *filial piety* cannot be reduced to financial maintenance? They may assert that if children will not take care of their parents even though they can afford to, then the State or the rest of society should foot the bill.

Such are the tensions behind this second principle.

PRINCIPLE THREE: MANY HELPING HANDS

The third principle underpinning Singapore's social safety net is Many Helping Hands. It is the Government's long-standing belief that "in helping the disadvantaged, everyone has the responsibility and an important aim is to foster a caring and compassionate society to encourage those who are more able to help those who are less able."[3]

Increasingly, service delivery and monitoring roles are outsourced to agencies like NCSS, family services centres and VWOs. The state has taken on the role of planner, policy-maker, and regulator, and also funds developmental and partial operating costs of selected service providers.

Many useful projects and initiatives have resulted from the "Many Helping Hands" approach. But this approach has often been challenged — not in terms of its spirit, but in terms of its effectiveness.

In my maiden parliament speech in November 2006, I expressed the need for this sacred cow to be sent for examination, to see if it ought to be

---

[3] Yap Mui Teng, Senior Research Fellow Institute of Policy Studies, Singapore, powerpoints, 2004.

slaughtered — or if it was at least due for a makeover, particularly in the area of the delivery of essential services to the disadvantaged. At the time, I was frustrated that services such as the education of special-needs students and the running of healthcare organisations such as the step-down community hospitals were led by charity organisations instead of the relevant government ministries.

I did not think that it was appropriate to leave the delivery of such essential services to charities whose board members were often too busy and distracted to focus on running these organisations. These charities, in turn, often had difficulty attracting qualified staff.

I also see a lack of co-ordination that has led to less than robust case management and co-ordination. Some clients are over-served, with multiple avenues for seeking help, while others are under-served. Some are not served at all, and fall through the cracks. I have observed that there is an inconsistent standard of service provisions. The prognoses of clients, young and old, is largely dependent on the varying degrees of commitment, competence and aspiration of each charity.

At the 2009 Committee of Supply debates, MPs expressed that the "Many Helping Hands" approach needed a "central mind to co-ordinate the efforts of different agencies," a database, and thorough case management to follow through on chronic cases.

Going forward with increasing pressure for results rather than schemes and activities, it is likely that the Many Helping Hands approach will be closely examined. Hopefully, the right hands would be deployed more effectively.

WHOSE JOB IS IT ANYWAY TO CREATE A CARING SOCIETY?

Whose job it is to create an inclusive and caring society and to ensure the disadvantaged are not left behind in meritocratic Singapore? If we conduct a straw poll among typical Singaporeans, the answer is likely to be: the Government.

GOVERNMENT

Indeed, the State has to play a leading role so that all individuals and groups, including those in the most marginalised communities, have equal access to the collective goods that are the citizen's basic social entitlement. It must be the role of the Government to strengthen the social safety net and to ensure that every citizen — not just those who are able and talented — partakes in the fruits of our country's growth. We are as good as our weakest link. If we do not commit to taking care of the weakest members of our society, fewer and fewer citizens will heed the call to procreate, lest they give birth to less than perfect children; or because their hope of getting out of the poverty cycle grows dimmer by the year.

At Government level, I believe in the need for a deeper study of our country's social safety net, particularly the principles behind who the safety net should catch and how it is cast. We should also identify the holes in the net and mend the gaping holes so that fewer people will fall through the holes.

In addition, the State must actively engage its citizens in developing and communicating the terms of the social contract, so that most citizens will enter and abide by it. There must be a better understanding and acceptance of the key principles that are good for the long-term survival of Singapore as a society; and what privileges should be considered basic rights of citizens without turning to unreasonable or unhealthy entitlement claims. As Dwight Eisenhower, the 34th President of the United States, once warned: "A people that values its privileges above its principles soon loses both."

But beyond the Government, each of us can do much more to make a difference in cultivating an inclusive and caring society. I believe that the real wealth of a country is when all stakeholders, not just politicians, businessmen and employers, take our place and play a role in developing a more caring society in everyday life.

ADVOCATES

Those of us who are advocates for our people or animals whose interests we passionately represent must first seek to understand. Only then we would stand a better chance of being heard and responded to. Only then there would be a higher probability that in the case of a stalemate, a creative third alternative can emerge.

In a neighbourhood where pigeons often congregate, residents who fear bird-related diseases insist that the pigeons be culled. Bird-lovers, on the other hand, continue to feed them and object to them being killed. Government agencies, wary of both parties, refrain from taking any action lest they become the ant on which the elephants trample.

Before coming to this conference, I received a very demanding and angry note from a disabled citizen, who insisted that Government is completely at fault for the current state of affairs in his life and community.

To be effective advocates, we need to understand the fine balance between courage and consideration. We must have the courage to identify the gaps, advocate for improvements, and shape services. However, we must also be wise and considerate, and learn to cite compelling cases so that others will want to support us. We must not only demand services, but, in most instances, be willing to become part of the solution. Some of the causes we fight for are at the initial stage of progress and others are at a more mature state. Some of our ideas may be ahead of times, so we need to be more patient and persuasive. Only then, our chances of being heard would increase and the solutions we propose would be supported and sustained beyond us.

INDIVIDUALS

As for the rest of Singaporeans, who are neither policy-makers, advocates nor the disadvantaged, I urge you to join in the journey to make our country a more inclusive and caring one. As Mahatma Gandhi put it, "We need to be the change that we want in the world."

"Treat others the way you expect to be treated"; "Love thy neighbour as thyself"; "Do unto others as you would have others do unto you" — so the wise sayings go.

Stop asking "what is in it for me?" But rather "how can I help?" Does not just rely on bashing others when things go wrong. Everyone can identify a problem — the real significance is how we can try to be part of the solution.

Each year, Singapore students with their Community Involvement Programmes (CIP) and Service Learning Plans hunt VWOs down with their favourite plans, telling others what they want to do and mostly forgetting to ask what their beneficiaries really need.

We have heard of the long queues for heavily subsidised Housing and Development Board (HDB) flats and desperate and angry applicants waiting their turns. It is, of course, the duty of the Government to meet the urgent needs of the homeless. At the same time, there are tenants who are no longer poor but insist they continue to stay in these subsidised flats because of their need for privacy or because they cannot bring themselves to give up such privileges, depriving those who are genuinely in need of low-cost housing.

Hence, in our efforts to build an inclusive and caring society, we need to put into practice what we preach, especially when it comes to respecting those whose social status are below ours or who are disadvantaged in some way.

In my work as an MP and as Chairperson of a Town Council, I have sometimes observed with angst how Singaporeans treat our cleaners and front-line officers. Few offer the words "sorry," "please," "thank you," or compliments when things go right.

CONCLUSION

In conclusion, we do not need to be policy-makers or regulators, or even be in politics, to make Singapore a more inclusive and caring society. Each of us can improve our society by thinking of and doing less for ourselves and our families, and more for others in our outer circles. Walk the extra mile. Arise from the seat of the armchair critic to really contribute. That way, Singapore can move one step close to a world in which everyone can potentially achieve the full measure of our humanity.

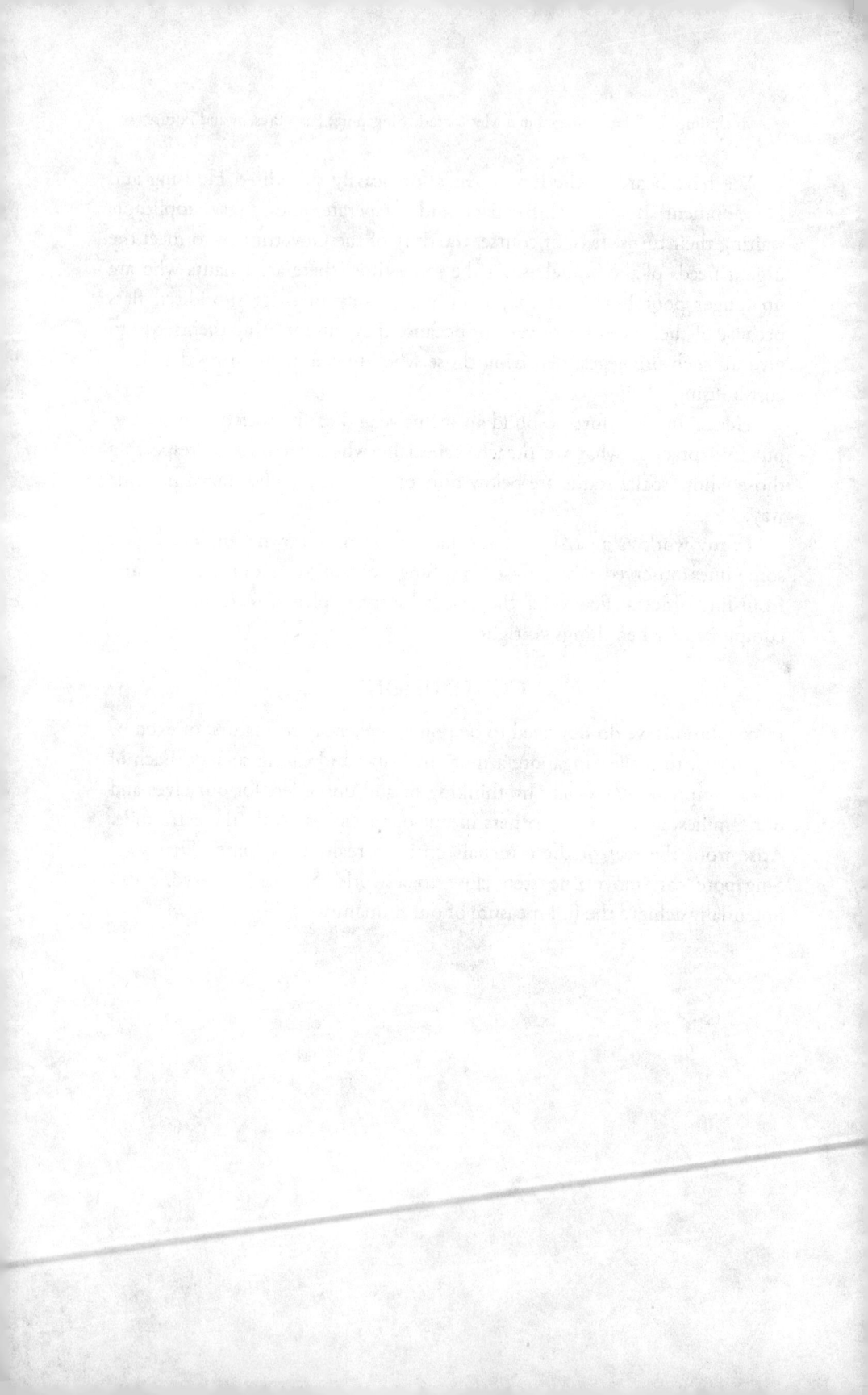

CHAPTER 6

Theatre is a Language

KOK HENG LEUN

THE CARING COMMUNITY

The website of the Ministry of Community Development, Youth and Sports defines a caring (and active) community as "one where the people, private, and public sector, bond together to help others, instead of relying solely on the public sector to support the needy."

Such a community provides a safety net — made of many helping hands — to those in need. In the process, strong bonds are formed between members of the community. "A community that bonds and cares is a pillar for harmonious living."[1]

In the same vein, the National Arts Council has advocated the use of the arts to bond the community.

However, a caring and active community must also be an empowered community. An empowered community possesses a collective imagination of what the community is now and what it can become in the possible future.

The community is constantly in search of its identity. This identity is not one that is prescribed, but rather one that evolves and changes over time. By excavating the memory of the community, the community begins to define what it is. But in the process of defining its identity, a community can become exclusive, thereby marginalising others.

---

[1] From the Ministry of Community Development.
<http://app1.mcys.gov.sg/AboutMCYS/OurFivePillars/ACaringandActiveCommunity.aspx>

An empowered community is one that is proud of what it is, and is also inclusive. The empowered community must be able to reflect and have the ability to observe what it is.

INVENTION OF THEATRE AS DEFINED BY AUGUSTO BOAL

Augusto Boal, a Brazilian theatre director and one of the most important theatre masters of this century, described how theatre was invented in his book *Rainbow of Desires*:

> "Theatre is the first human invention and also the invention which paves the way for all other inventions and discoveries.
>
> Theatre is born when the human being discovers that it can observe itself; when it discovers that, in this act of seeing, it can see itself — see itself in situ: see itself seeing.
>
> Observing itself, the human being perceives what it is, discovers what it is not and imagines what it could become. It perceives where it is and where it is not, and imagines where it could go."

So, you see, the essence of theatre is about observing oneself. The human being not only "makes" theatre — it is theatre.

As the 17th century Spanish poet and playwright Lope de Vega put it:

> "Theatre is two human beings, a passion and a platform."

Theatre is the passionate combat of two human beings on a platform. We are looking at how human beings relate with

> another human;
> with society; and
> with self.

When we watch theatre, it is through this aesthetic space that we see ourselves. When we make theatre, we are also creating the aesthetic space to understand ourselves. In the same way, when the community makes theatre, it is trying to understand its identity.

The community tells its story through theatre. These stories are memories of the past, lessons of the past, created based on the experience of the community. However it is also an imaginative re-telling of the past. Sometimes, it also provides imaginative possibilities for the past. Theatre activates the imagination of the maker and the people who watch it.

Memory gives us a sense of who we are. Imagination gives us hope for the future.

THE EMPOWERED SPECTATOR: SPECT-ACTOR

In conventional theatre, the theatre artists make the proposition and present them on stage. They propose what makes up the memories of the community, and also make imaginative propositions about the future. But can the spectator also be empowered? Can they also share their memories and make propositions?

Forum theatre is a technique developed by Augusto Boal, which transforms the passive spectator into an active spect-actor.

It first shows a piece of theatre, called an "anti-model," which depicts an issue that needs to be dealt with, but which has been mishandled and thus resolved tragically. A dialogue is then created with the spectator, to discuss how the issue can best be dealt with.

The spectactor is an empowered spectator. The empowered spectator does not want to sit passively and be told what happens next; the empowered spectator acts and participates in the making of theatre.

In forum theatre, the empowered spectators empathise with the struggle on stage, and then imagine propositions in order to make changes, act on the imagination, and reflect.

Hence, a spect-actor is a critical learner who is not only reflective but also has empathy. Through theatre, the spect-actor sees itself *in situ*, and then rehearses the possibilities of what it can be through the safe space of theatre.

COMMUNITY MAKING THEATRE

In forum theatre, the audience also makes theatre. Each intervention from the audience evolves into new dramaturgy. In this space, everyone can imagine, everyone can make theatre. Hence, this form of theatre is very effective in building an empowered and caring community.

The community makes theatre not only to bond, but also to find what makes this community unique and, at the same time, reflect upon what this community can be. It is not just about bonding — it is about being open and inclusive.

By making theatre, and engaging in a dialogue with the community, we see what we represent and evaluate what we represent.

But we do not stay alive in the comfort of nostalgia or familiarity. Rather, we cross boundaries and borders, to understand, to be inclusive, because we know we are an evolving community.

We then make imaginative interventions to rehearse what can be possible, and remember to constantly reflect.

When community makes theatre, it can transform itself constantly, from a passive entity into an active and caring one.

When community makes theatre, it partakes in a humanizing process.

THEATRE IS A LANGUAGE

As can be seen from the discussion so far, theatre is dialogic. It is a system of communication that does not just use words, but also actions, reflections, imagination, and memory. Theatre wants human beings to understand one another, in order to bring forth ideas and make interventions.

Theatre is a language that encourages participation, dialogue, remembering, and imagination.

Most importantly, it is a communication system that happens when members in the audience put aside their daily chores, work, and other worldly commitments. The audience sets aside this time to enjoy, to think and to act. And time is what we need as human beings. We have forgotten to stop, forgotten to give space for ourselves, and for others.

During the past 25 years, a new perspective on life has evolved. This perspective is different from the mechanistic view of Descartes and Newton.

This new paradigm is more holistic, and ecological. It is a world that is not so materialistic — it is concerned with a complex network of relationships.

Fritjof Capra suggested this:

> "Evolution is no longer seen as a competitive struggle for existence, but rather a cooperative dance in which creativity and the constant drive for novelty are the driving forces."

Perhaps we should discard the rhetoric of competition, which has done much harm to our earth.

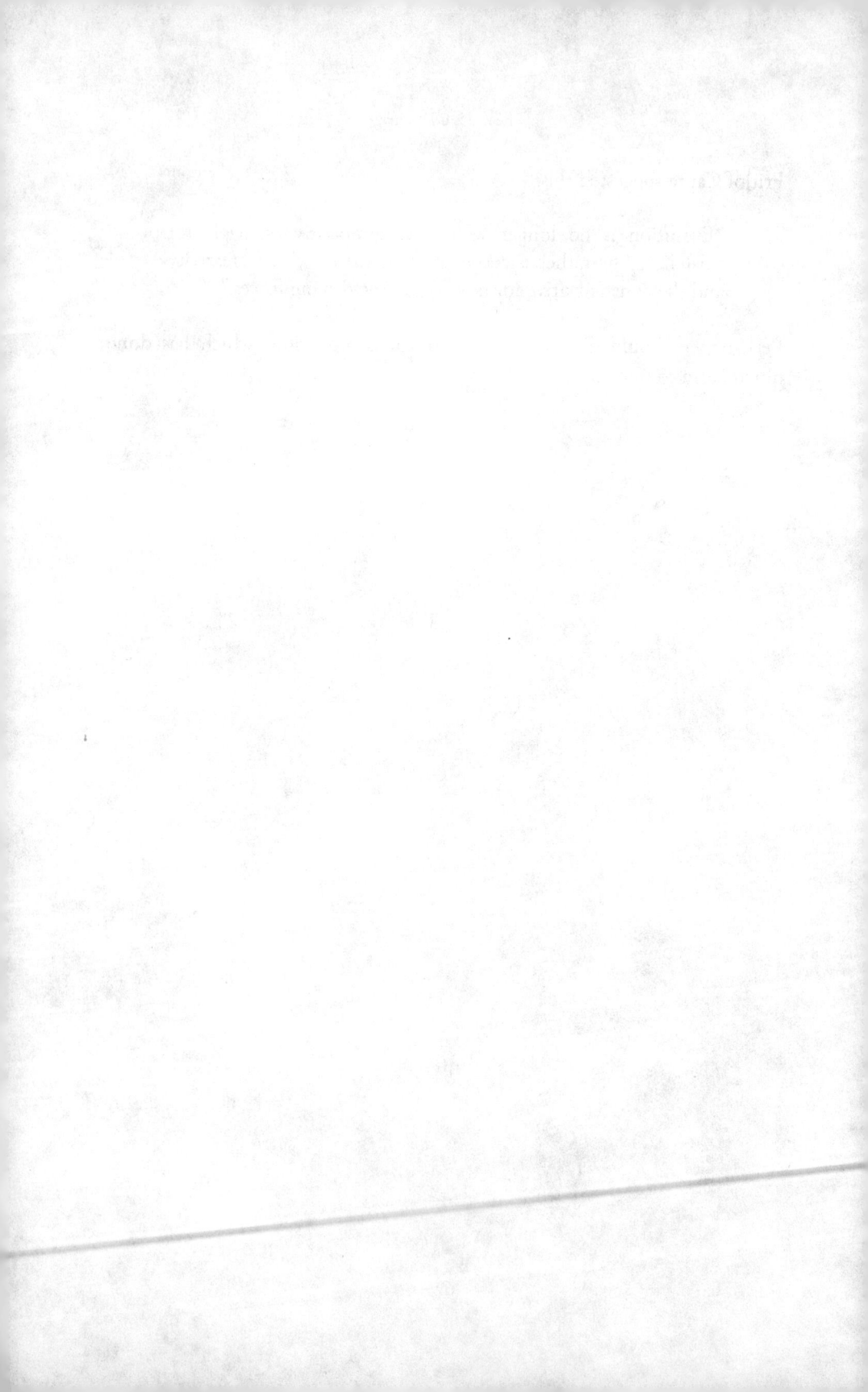

DISCUSSANT NOTES

T. K. UDAIRAM
Panel on Caring Community

The following are the key points from the three presentations about "Caring Community."

Singaporeans, in general, are a caring group. As President of Mercy Relief, I have seen Singaporeans responding generously whenever help is needed. In response to the 2006 tsunami, for example, Singaporeans donated both money and time to help with disaster relief efforts.

But tensions exist between volunteerism and the fast pace of life in Singapore. Donations are perhaps the best thing that Singaporeans can do for charity, given their resources, opportunities, and needs. The question for Singapore's Voluntary Welfare Organisations (VWOs) is whether they are able to utilise the time of their volunteers effectively.

Singapore does not have a significant underclass. In fact, the underclass has been well taken care of by government schemes. It is not the underclass that has problems in coping with their lives, but the middle class that is struggling to keep up.

Lastly, Singapore's civil society has not been able to develop at the same speed as the country's development from Third World to First World. Civil society should not be dependent on the government to take action on social issues; instead, civil society should develop and grow so that it can take the lead at times.

IV

Singapore Spirit

In his National Day Rally speech in 2010, Prime Minister Lee Hsien Loong spoke about the Singapore Spirit, which is based on shared experiences and values, a commitment to the nation, and the common dreams and aspirations of its citizens. The

Singapore identity, though visible, is also a work-in-progress. One main concern has been, and continues to be: How can we build up an enhanced sense of belonging and rootedness, particularly as Singapore becomes a more diverse and open country? Can we do more to foster a shared sense of association to place, heritage, and history? How do we keep Singaporeans at home and abroad connected and involved in local issues, and strengthen their national identity? An endearing home, with familiar public symbols and good memories, is essential for harnessing the Singapore Spirit. How do we take advantage of new media and technology to facilitate person-to-person connectivity? It has been argued that community bonding has a direct relationship with the level of social trust and civic engagement, which covers a broad spectrum of activities such as voluntary work, activism and the delivery of social services by non-government actors.

How can we refine our structures and processes to deepen such engagement?

CHAPTER 7

The Singapore Spirit: An Immigrant's Perspective

ORI SASSON

ABSTRACT

National identity in a globalised world is a complex issue. In the case of Singapore, this complexity is exacerbated by the immense diversity of the population, as well as the fact that Singapore is a young nation.

To the outsider, the Singapore identity offers multiple paradoxes. For example, the narrative of hard work as the recipe for success is inculcated from a young age. Yet, various forms of lottery and "lucky draws" are extremely popular. Similarly, one of the most commonly cited national traits is being *kiasu* (literally, "scared to lose"). Yet, people are often complacent enough to use their mobile phones to "reserve" tables in food courts.

The notion of the Singapore Spirit as described by Prime Minister Lee Hsien Loong in the National Day Rally 2010 creates a vision of national identity that is focused more on the future than on the past.

This is fitting for a young nation of citizens who are mostly the descendents of immigrants who may not share a long common history. Together with the notions of meritocracy and multi-racialism, this Singapore Spirit creates a non-ethnic national narrative which would be attractive to individuals from every possible background, and even more so for talented ones. But such a national narrative carries one major risk, which relates to its resilience, or ability to withstand severe shock, internal or external.

Still, a national narrative focused on the future is really "uniquely Singapore." It also serves a practical purpose in that it has the distinct potential to create a bright future for Singapore.

INTRODUCTION

National identity in a globalised world is a complex issue, especially in countries with a significant population of migrants. In some nations, migrants may need to fit into an existing national narrative. But Singapore's national narrative is not as clearly established as that of other nations. This is both due to the nation being relatively young, as well as the multi-racial, multi-cultural, and multi-religious nature of Singapore's population. The large number of foreign workers, immigrants, and tourists makes the national narrative even more elusive. A typical Singaporean individual may spend a large part of her time surrounded by non-Singaporeans.

This paper addresses the notion of the Singapore national identity and the Singapore Spirit from an immigrant's perspective. It starts by highlighting several paradoxes in the Singapore identity, followed by a short discussion about the official narrative of the Singapore Spirit as described by Prime Minister Lee Hsien Loong. It ends with more personal views on the Singapore national narrative.

WHAT DOES IT MEAN TO BE SINGAPOREAN?

If one conducts an open-ended survey asking Singaporeans what it means to be Singaporean, there will probably be a wide range of answers, and many of the answers may not be relevant for all Singaporeans.

For example, one may answer that "serving National Service (NS)" means that you are Singaporean. But second-generation Permanent Residents (PRs) do in fact serve NS; and female and first-generation new citizens do not.

Another person may try to characterise Singaporeans by their love of a particular type of hawker fare. Yet, this same food may also be served across the causeway in Malaysia.

From the perspective of an outsider who first visited Singapore in 1994, before moving to Singapore in 2002, I have always felt that there are multiple paradoxes in the definition of the traits of Singaporeans.

Complaining, Eating, and Shopping

In my first few visits to Singapore, my impression was that the identifying traits of Singaporeans are complaining, eating, and shopping. My first visit in 1994 happened soon after the introduction of the Goods and Services Tax (GST). Everyone, from shop-owners and taxi drives to consumers, were quick to explain how wrong the tax was. Coming from Israel, where the equivalent tax (called VAT) stood at 17%, and having travelled to many other countries, my personal view was that 3% was a low rate.

Other typical complaints I heard were about bosses scolding their staff, or general views about the difficulty of work (e.g. "this thing very *jialat*").

As a visitor, I quickly learned that eating and shopping were widely viewed as national traits. My hosts were always proud to bring me to new places to try new types of food, and were very happy with my willingness to try different types of food. Staying at a hotel in Orchard Road, I could not avoid visiting shopping malls over the weekend, which were all crowded with shoppers. I later learned that crowded shopping malls do not represent the pinnacle of crowdedness. Avid shoppers always look for "good deals," so the ultimate crowded shopping experience would be going to one of Singapore's information technology (IT) shows.

As I began to visit Singapore more frequently, I often read *The Straits Times*. From *The Straits Times*, I learnt other defining traits of Singaporeans, such as being *kiasu* ("scared to lose"), *kiasi* ("scared to die"), and the pursuit of the "5 Cs" (Cash, Car, Condo, Club, Credit Card).

Paradox One: Hard Work versus Lucky Draw

The more time I spent in Singapore, the more I realised that many facets of the Singaporean identity are paradoxes. Such paradoxes can be explained in various ways: the result of the clash of Eastern and Western cultures and values; the result of "social engineering" by the Government; or the result if a diverse population. But even with such explanations, a paradox adds complexity to the national identity and national narratives.

One example of such a paradox is the national narrative of hard work on the one hand, versus the love of various forms of lucky draws on the other. The national narrative of hard work is well established, and the narrative of hard work as a recipe for success is inculcated from a young age. According to this narrative, those who have good grades will be granted scholarships, and will subsequently land coveted jobs.

Similarly, statistics show that the number of hours worked per week in Singapore is relatively high compared to other countries. Yet, while hard work is strongly emphasised, there is a strong "Lucky Draw" narrative which appears contradictory.

This lucky draw is visible in advertisements ("buy XYZ and stand to win ABC"), in events held by grassroots organisations (where often there is an early-bird lucky draw, grand lucky draw, and final lucky draw) and in the popularity of 4D and Toto.

At first, I found the popularity of 4D fascinating, particularly the fact that people looked for lucky numbers everywhere. For example, when you have a newborn baby, people will ask what the newborn's weight is so they can use the numbers for 4D. Or if someone they know has bought a new car, they will quickly write down the license plate number to use it for 4D.

Paradox Two: Conformity versus Desire to Excel

As mentioned above, children are encouraged from a young age to excel in school, as this is the formula for success. Yet this desire to excel and the competitiveness it brings forth co-exist with a strong desire to conform to social norms and not to "stand out."

For instance, someone who is working extra-hard in the workplace will be viewed as "spoiling the market," even though everyone wants to reap the rewards of the same hard work.

Paradox Three: Scared to Lose, but not the Mobile Phone

One of the mostly commonly cited traits of Singaporeans is being *kiasu* ("scared to lose"). This trait has many manifestations, which are mostly competitive. For example, a *kiasu* person will not want to pay more for something than what someone else did, or not get the same benefits as someone else. This trait stands at odds with a very common Singaporean trait, which is a form of complacency. This complacency is manifested in the willingness of people who try to reserve tables in a food court or hawker centre using their mobile phones.

Paradox Four: World Class... or Are We?

One of the most interesting traits of Singaporeans which I have observed is the reluctance to be proud of the achievements of Singapore. I personally feel this almost every day, as people are not typically willing to believe I am a Singapore citizen. They appear to assume that whatever citizenship I had is better than a Singapore one, and thus it is illogical that I would have given up that citizenship to become a Singaporean. As a result, I have developed a habit of showing my identity card (IC) to strangers, even large crowds, as proof of my citizenship.

From a larger perspective, Singaporeans are often reluctant to accept that for many, life in Singapore is better than in Western countries such as Australia, the United Kingdom or the United States of America (USA). This is obvious judging by the number of expatriates from such countries who are keen to stay in Singapore, even on what is called "local terms" — without the benefits of an "expat package" in their remuneration packages.

The attraction of Singapore is that it offers economic opportunities, a safe and low-crime environment, a low tax rate, and conveniences such the efficiency of various agencies, and the affordability of foreign domestic workers, which may not be available in Western countries.

THE SINGAPORE SPIRIT

In the National Day Rally 2010, Prime Minister Lee Hsien Loong characterised the Singapore Spirit as being based on:

> "Deeper things which we share, shared values like multi-racialism or meritocracy or respect for every talent; shared loyalty and commitment to Singapore; shared responsibility for each other and pride in what we have done together; shared memories as well as dreams and aspirations."

He also characterised the Singapore Spirit as being:

"The determination that makes us press on when things are tough, like in the recession last year, the trust that keeps us together when forces try to pull us apart, like when we encountered extremist terrorism after 9/11. It is the competence and the quiet pride and discipline that make sure that things go right, like when we hosted the YOG. It is a confidence that we will prevail come what may. It is this spirit in each of us which makes Singapore work the way it does and which makes Singaporeans special."

This definition creates a vision of national identity that is more focused on the future than on the past. This is very different from other countries, where the national identity may have been forged over hundreds of years and, as such, would focus more on the past than the future.

This definition of the Singapore Spirit is fitting for a young nation of immigrants who may not share a long common history. It also makes it easier for a wider range of individuals to identify with this definition, as it creates a non-ethnic national narrative which would be attractive to individuals from every possible background, and even more so for talented ones. As such, it gels well with the notions of meritocracy and multi-racialism.

In making such a definition, there is an apparent trade-off between "casting a wide net" and creating a specific and emotion-evoking narrative. As the net is cast wider, the narrative becomes less specific. In other words, the more inclusive this narrative is, the larger the number of people who can relate to it, but perhaps not as strongly. For example, as the narrative becomes more inclusive, it could actually apply to non-Singaporeans, and in a sense "dilute" the fact it is a national narrative.

In particular, one risk that such a national narrative carries relates to resilience, or the ability to withstand severe shocks, internal or external. It is not certain how fragile this narrative might be in the face of severe challenges. However, given the experiences of the last decade or so, with 9/11, SARS, and the financial crisis, it appears that Singapore society is resilient enough to withstand shocks.

CONCLUSION

From a personal perspective, the "official" Singapore national narrative offers two major draws for newcomers. On one hand, it is a "work in progress," and as such is not yet fixed in a way that may exclude newcomers. On the other hand, it emphasises the notion of meritocracy and multi-racial and multi-religious co-existence, which are attractive to newcomers.

This national narrative is focused on the future. As such, I feel it is really "uniquely Singapore." It also serves a practical purpose in that it has the distinct potential to create a bright future for Singapore, because it rallies people around the goal of creating a better future for all Singaporeans and their families.

I believe there is still a gap in propagating this "official" narrative to the population, in terms of developing pride in being Singaporeans, or even having the "confidence we will prevail whatever may come."

However, my view is that there is a distinct Singaporean identity, as much as it is a "work in progress." It is difficult to characterise in terms of specific daily activities, since many non-Singaporean participate in such common activities, ranging from dining at a hawker centre to participating in grassroots activities. Similarly, a person may be only resident in Singapore, yet still be proud of Singapore.

Ironically, some distinct Singaporean traits, such as "Singlish," are opposed by the "official" narrative (as manifested in the "Speak Good English" campaign, or the "Speak Mandarin" campaign).

The fact that the Singapore narrative or identity can attract non-Singaporeans may be viewed as a disadvantage by some, but it does have the obvious advantage of attracting non-Singaporeans to become citizens, thus countering the low fertility rate among Singaporeans.

As mentioned above, a key risk to the Singapore narrative is its resilience. For example, souring social mood and economic contraction might make it difficult to maintain an inclusive narrative, as individuals look for someone to blame. However, given the experience of the past decade, it appears that Singapore is able to deal with a rapidly changing environment despite being a young nation.

To conclude, it is worth highlighting that no discussion of the Singapore identity is complete without mentioning the Singapore political system.

With a single dominant party in power since independence, it is difficult to untangle the official narrative of the Singapore identity from the values of the ruling People's Action Party (which include, for example, meritocracy and multi-racialism).

Furthermore, a large part of the Singapore identity relates to another paradox: A seemingly ambivalent relationship with the government. Without going into specific political issues, this paradox relates to the notion of the "Nanny State." It is common to hear calls for less government involvement in various aspects of life. But, at the same time, the Government is expected to be omnipotent and help individuals cope with difficulties ranging from inflation to economic contractions.

CHAPTER 8

The Singapore Spirit is not a Pontianak — What is it?

WOFFLES WU

Ambassador Ong Keng Yong, distinguished guests:

When I accepted the invitation to speak at this prestigious forum, I had no idea I would be so far out of my depth. I am neither a politician nor an academic. Travelling around the world to deliver lectures on plastic surgery is easy, as I know the topic well. But putting my thoughts together and wrapping my head around, a topic as intangible as the "Singapore Spirit," has been a challenge for me.

After reading *Singapore Perspectives* 2010, I realised that everything that needs to be said and discussed has already been covered by personalities more qualified than myself. Our Prime Minister, professors, political scientists, policy makers, and sociologists have succinctly and cogently spoken their minds on what Singapore is about, the direction it is headed in, and how this is to be achieved.

What can I possibly contribute to this forum? Have I been asked to speak because I am an artist, an actor, a failed restaurateur, a film-maker, a writer, or someone who is just passionate about the arts and heritage of Singapore? Is it because of my contributions as a doctor to the patients I serve and to the international world of plastic surgery? Or is it because being international in outlook, I get to observe Singapore from various angles?

I felt that the only way I could contribute meaningfully is to give my own perspective of why Singapore is my home and what it means to me, having grown up and made a career for myself here. I also wish to highlight the various people and talents whom I have been associated with and who I think have made Singapore the vibrant metropolis it is now. These individuals are living the Singapore Dream.

First, what is the "Singapore Spirit"? Is it like the Christmas Spirit, which celebrates family, fellowship, good cheer, the giving of presents, a time of worship, and a time to consider the less fortunate? Can we define it in similar terms?

To me the "Singapore Spirit" is about many things — some more immediately apparent than others. It is about the qualities and the drive that has enabled us to make a successful transformation from Third World to First World status in such a short span of time. This is founded on our "never say die, anything can be done" attitude and our belief that we can achieve anything.

It is this strong belief that we control our own destiny that has given us the confidence to go head to head with any country or body on a variety of issues. We have our political forefathers to thank for instilling in us this self-belief, and for providing us with the platform to springboard forward. But we also need to credit, as a people, our collective endurance, hard work, and our ability to change and adapt to new situations.

We also need to be mindful that the "Singapore Spirit" has a flip side and can manifest itself in negative ways. We must not be blinded by success and become cocky and arrogant, unfeeling, uncharitable, opportunistic, or eager to benefit from the misfortune of others.

We have to be less "kiasu" (Hokkien for "scared to lose") and curb our desire to win or benefit at all times. Queuing overnight to buy a condominium in order to resell it that very day or queuing for hours at a petrol station to get an additional 5% discount are laughable examples of this behaviour. But selfishly occupying public transport seats meant for the elderly and pregnant women or parking in handicap lots are a more disturbing manifestation of the "me first!" generation. Our society still needs to be guided and moulded in order to become more gracious and caring of others.

When I lecture or conduct surgeries overseas, I am often asked why I do not choose to live in London, New York, or Paris. Would I be not more successful in any of these great capitals of the world, have more patients, earn more, and have a better life? Would my star not burn brighter overseas?

The question is well-intended but it is based on a lack of knowledge of what Singapore has to offer and end up being condescending.

The answer is an emphatic NO. Why would I want to live in any of these places when I can live in Singapore?

In the 1950s and 60s, a young plastic surgeon named Ivo Pitanguy living in Rio de Janeiro in Brazil made a name for himself by pioneering several plastic surgery procedures. Soon patients, students, and fellows flocked from around the world to Brazil, bypassing the more traditional locations in the United States, and making Brazil a tourist destination and a plastic surgery hotspot. To this day, Pitanguy remains in Rio. He is proud that his achievements have contributed to the vitality and legend of Rio.

Our own Dr Arthur Lim has done the same thing for ophthalmology and put us on the international map.

My aspiration is to contribute in a similar way to plastic surgery, and to Singapore, as we become an international medical hub. I would like patients and students to come to me, and not me to them. I would like this to be my hub. I am in my comfort zone here.

This has required much groundwork over the past 15 years, during which I have travelled the world extensively, teaching, operating, establishing professional networks, and forging those invisible links with like-minded colleagues who believe in the highest standards of professionalism and results. International colleagues now have the confidence to send their patients to me here in Singapore. The hard work has paid off.

In my own way, like many others, I try to do the best for myself and my patients, my family, the community I belong to, and, if possible, my country. If I can contribute on an international level, it is a bonus and a privilege. Success means different things to each of us and some set their targets higher than others. No matter what level of success we attain, these are all positive contributions to the growth and prosperity of our country.

Some of us are cogs in the wheel, some are the wheels. But each component is indispensable, no matter how small it is.

I love Singapore. I do not love everything about it though. Certainly not the selfish behaviour — the *kiasu* behaviour I mentioned earlier — the terrible toilets, the rude, and dangerous drivers, the fact that we never greet our neighbours or say good morning in the lift.

I dislike some government policies, like scrapping cars that are more than ten years old, needing a Certificate of Entitlement (COE) in order to have a car, or paying Electronic Road Pricing surcharges at 10.30pm when Singaporeans tired from a day at work are rushing home to see their families or to rest. Clamping down on the official use of dialects when many citizens still speak dialect to communicate in a more intimate way is another pet peeve. I am aware why some of these policies are in effect, as they serve a greater good, but they often appear overly restrictive and punitive. Living in our version of Utopia has a price to pay but I still would not want to live anywhere else.

I have loved Singapore from the time it was a sleepy hollow. I still love it now, as it has transformed into an exciting, entertaining, and multifaceted cosmopolitan city, which offers everything from a safe business environment to excellent dining at all levels, superb education and an arts and cultural scene that rivals any Western country.

I travel every month. It is interesting to visit new countries, but after a few days away I cannot wait to board the Singapore Airlines plane that will take me back to Singapore, the land where almost everything works. Once I see the friendly smiles of the crew members, read my *The Straits Times* and order cup noodles, the stress of travel leaves me and I feel a tremendous sense of relief.

Singapore has transformed beyond recognition. Our physical environment, the cityscape, the clever town planning and the innovative architecture has allowed us to become one of the most beautiful cities in the world.

Just a few nights ago, as I sat in the gorgeously restored Collyer Quay (now the Fullerton Bay Hotel) gazing across the Marina at Marina Bay Sands, I was stunned by the scale, magnificence, and beauty of the vista before me. I felt I was in the middle of an illuminated jewel box that rivalled the splendour of anything in London, Paris, Barcelona, or New

York. I told my foreign guests, who were here for Art Stage Singapore, that they were looking at Singapore at the peak of its development, the fruition of many years of planning and investment.

But it was not always like this.

When I was growing up in the 1960s and 70s, Singapore was still in its infancy as a nation. Chinatown was still a mass of people in dilapidated shop-houses, the Singapore River was a cauldron of debris and decay and bumboats lined up choc a bloc with stench to match. Traffic was sparse, a Mercedes Benz 280s cost $18,000 and bungalows were under $100,000.

Our biggest tourist attraction was the transvestites of Bugis Street and our most famous medical export was Professor Ratnam, who made Singapore the international hub of sex-change operations, long before Bangkok came into the picture. The bar at the Mitre Hotel was a crowd favourite with expats and locals on a shoestring budget and the Raffles Hotel was at its most decrepit state, all shabby and worn out.

Then things started to change rapidly. If we wanted to be plugged into the world's economy and become a First World country, we needed better infrastructure and operating systems in our quest to become a financial hub and the Switzerland of Asia. We needed a better city-scape, better tourist attractions and we needed to modernise. That we achieved this in a few short years is legendary and I will not dwell on these successes. The spirit of entrepreneurship and efficiency is a key component of the "Singapore Spirit" and we all know this.

But the success of a country does not rest only on its financial achievements or in the fact that we have provided a roof over everyone's heads. Once the basic necessities have been accounted for, a nation needs to develop a soul and to develop many layers of diversity to make life interesting and multi-faceted. This creates a place for people of different levels and backgrounds, different jobs, hobbies, lifestyle choices and allows us to meld and grow with one another. This is the spirit of tolerance and acceptance.

As teenagers, we all wanted to travel to Europe and the United States for further education or just to soak up the sights and sounds of countries with hundreds of years of culture and history. We were exposed to colourful lifestyles, different societies and were able to bring these influences back to Singapore to create our own versions of a modern Asian lifestyle.

I want to highlight the creative talents and the pioneers of the softscape who have enriched our social landscape and made Singapore a fun and exciting place to live in. This is not just about mainstream art and culture, but also about those who improve our lifestyle choices and add colour and diversity to our lives. These are the fashion designers, interior designers, creative directors, hairdressers, stylists, make-up artists, theatre practitioners, photographers, artists, gallery owners, film-makers, dancers, musicians, boutique owners, restaurateurs, disco and pub owners, furniture store owners, hobbyists, those involved in Chinese opera, Indian classical dance, Malay arts, ballet, and so many other different jobs and shops. They embody the spirit of creativity.

Even the old man in Arab Street selling beads and sequins, or the junk store owner Ah Keng who sells old, used furniture, are important parts of this aspect of our development, because they epitomize the spirit of creativity and fun and daring. Daring to live their lives in unconventional jobs or vocations, daring to show others that they can survive, that it can be done their way. They are our mavericks. They give us inspiration.

We owe a debt of gratitude to the pioneers who walked before us.

Before David Gan became a household name in hairdressing, there was Willie's of London at Tanglin Shopping Centre and the famous Roland Chow of Orchard Road. Before Takashimaya, we had Chotirmall, Melwani's, Khemco and C. K. Tang. Before X-tra, Space and other high-end furniture stores, there was Diethelm and Van Hin the local furniture maker.

Long before Stephanie Sun and J. J. Lin came onto the scene, there were the talented Anita Sarawak, Dick Lee, Chris Ho, and Jacintha Abisheganaden plugging away in the music industry. Tony, Terry and Spencer and Mathew and the Mandarins were just two of the music groups that originated in the 1970s and went on to attain international recognition. Long before drag queen Kumar became popular and acceptable, there was the irrepressible band Tania in the Hilton Hotel Lobby Bar, with their cross-dressing lead singer Alban.

Before there was Ashley Isham, we had Tan Yoong and Bobby Chng. Goh Poh Seng, a fellow doctor, started several arts-related food and beverage outlets that became hubs for creative types. First, there was *Bistro Toulouse Lautrec*, at the back of Tanglin Shopping Centre, where Tania subsequently moved to; and then the *Rainbow Lounge* in the same vicinity. Jacintha had her first solo concert there in 1982, singing songs from her debut album *Silence*. Many of her songs were produced by a young medical doctor, Dr Sydney Tan, who would later produce many songs and albums for local and international singers. He also wrote the musical score for the internationally released feature film *Singapore Dreaming*, which I co-produced in 2007.

I was lucky to be part of that creative group. In the 1970s, I used to play football with my neighbour and Jacintha's brother Peter Abisheganaden. I later took double bass and guitar lessons from their father Alex Abisheganaden, the guitar maestro. Dick Lee would often come to the house, as would other singers of the day, so it was an extremely creative environment to grow up in.

In 1977, Pat Chan, our swimming princess and multi-medalist at the SEA Games, turned her attention to producing a musical called "*Stardust.*" This was a seminal and ground-breaking event because there had never been a musical of this scale featuring local performers before.

Held in the DBS Auditorium, the diverse cast hailed from all walks of life and this musical was to prove a springboard for many of them. Pat Chan, her brothers Mark and Roy (all National swimmers), Jacintha, Siva Choy, Wilson David, Moe Alkaff, Betty Khoo (the editor of *Female*), Terry Tan (who later became a celebrity chef in London), Winston Tan from the advertising industry, journalist Irene Hoe, Gerry Rezel, and Bob Fernandes (Singapore's James Ingram) were all part of this. At 17, I was the youngest singer and dancer in the group. New York-trained Gerald Chan choreographed our dance steps.

I remember in 1989 watching with pride the acclaimed play *M. Butterfly* at London's Drury Lane Theatre, where a young Glen Goei acted with the famed Sir Anthony Hopkins. Glen could have stayed on in London, but chose to return to Singapore to contribute to the diversity of local theatre. He has been responsible for numerous films and theatrical productions. Together with practitioners from TheatreWorks, The Necessary Stage and groups like the Dim Sum Dollies, we have developed our own brand of theatre and unique humour. Without these Singaporeans, who followed their passions and dared to live their lives differently, we would not have the vibrant city of today.

In fashion, daring individuals like Christina Ong, Farah Khan (then known as Kheng Lin) and Tina Tan paved the way, bringing in high-end fashion that made Singapore more interesting. Man and His Woman, the Link Boutique, Club 21, and other fashion stores offered variety beyond the safety of Robinson's, OG and Metro. In the early 1980s, Tina Tan opened the first Gianni Versace shop in the world outside of Italy. It was quite a coup to have beaten London, New York, Paris, Rome, and Tokyo for this honour. This in turn supported the modelling industry, which allowed agencies like Mannequin studios, Imp international and Carrie Models to grow from strength to strength. Carrie Models was started by Carrie Wong in a small office in the basement car park of the Hyatt Hotel in 1976. Brandon Barker, Dick Lee, and Linda Teo all contributed to its early success. Carrie Models is now international and has branches in Singapore, Malaysia, Hong Kong, and China. Even older than the Government Investment Corporation of Singapore (GIC), they will be celebrating their 35th anniversary this year.

In photography, before Chuando, David Tan, and John Clang, there were the likes of celebrity photographer Willie Tang and Russell Wong, who became famous after his glorious shot of Sebastian Coe was used for the cover of *Sports Illustrated*. When we were teenagers in the 1970s, I used to take photos with Russell and developed these photos in the bathtub of his Katong home.

In 1975, Jean Yip and Mervin Wee met. They were 16-year-old drop-outs who shared a love for hairstyling, and were armed only with ambition and guts. They went to London to train, honed their skills, brought these back to Singapore and started the Jean Yip chain of hair and beauty salons. They have never looked back. Today, with 66 branches in Singapore and Malaysia, they are living the Singapore Dream. They give back to the community by imparting their hair and business skills to young students and staff at their training centre, and by providing jobs to more than 1,000 people. It is amazing what hard work, determination, and talent can achieve.

This is just a small sampling of interesting individuals who have added colour and texture to our social fabric, and who have shown us their "Singapore Spirit." They paved the way for the success of today's entrepreneurs, with their beautiful boutiques, mega-salons, photography and film studios, which are able to live off the music, entertainment, beauty, and lifestyle industry.

We should remember that every time a Singaporean becomes successful internationally, be in the fields of commerce, business, sports, the arts, or sciences, it is not just a personal success but also a success for our country. It paves the way for others to follow. The "Singapore Spirit" is our collective spirit. It is the SPIRIT of SINGAPORE. Boomz!!

9

Localism versus Globalism

JANADAS DEVAN

I visited a place called Little Gidding a couple of years ago, a tiny village in Cambridgeshire, England. It was difficult to find even with a Global Positioning System (GPS) device.

Nicholas Ferrar and his family had established a religious community there in 1626 and the poet T.S. Eliot had visited it 300 years later in 1936.

"If you come this way taking the route, you would be likely to take from the place you would be likely to come from...It would be the same," Eliot wrote in Little Gidding, the concluding poem in his magnum opus the *Four Quartets*.

"When you leave the rough road," "turn behind the pig-sty," walk round the hedges ("White again, in May, with voluptuary sweetness"), you would find, as always, "the dull facade and the tombstone."

I saw the tombstone — Ferrar's. I saw the dull facade — a small church that can seat no more than 30, built first in the 13th century, reconstructed in the 17th and repaired several times since. I saw the hedges. And I saw the pig-sty, now an all-purpose storehouse, with a motor-cycle in it.

Memory — personal, historical, and national — is always present in old countries like England; and even more so in ancient civilizations like China or India. Nostalgia in these lands, where the past lies thick on the ground, can readily find adequate objective correlatives for its yearnings.

Not so in Singapore.

Someone sent me a series of snapshots of "Old Singapore" about two years ago, around the time I visited Little Gidding. They were not of a particularly old Singapore, actually. The photos were of places and scenes and prospects that once existed within my lifetime, but are now no more: Queen Elizabeth Walk — not recognisable; National Theatre — demolished; Change Alley — changed beyond recognition.

My own personal memory is similarly bereft of stable external markers.

The houses I grew up in on Coronation Road — first an atap house and then a bungalow — have gone. The road I knew so well still wends its way along more or less the same path as it did 50 years ago, but past very different scenes. The Malay kampong folk, the Chinese shopkeepers, the Indian cowherds have made way for a string of semi- and detached bungalows, not all of them in good taste.

The school I attended, Anglo-Chinese School at Barker Road, does not look anything like it used to be; Safti has been transformed beyond recognition; the fields of the old Bukit Timah campus have been swallowed by the Botanic Gardens; Times House along Kim Seng Road has been obliterated.

About the only constructions in my personal memory that still look more or less the way they did when I first saw them are, strangely enough, Changi Prison — which I first saw as a child, visiting my father, when he was a political prisoner in the 1950s — and Conference Hall in Shenton Way, which used to be the headquarters of the National Trades Union Congress. I was very happy when they designated it a national monument the other day, and thus preserved it from obliteration.

If you came this way, taking the route you would be likely to take, from the place you would be likely to come from, it would almost invariably not be the same in Singapore.

It is difficult, almost impossible, to be nostalgic in this country, for its landscape is dotted with precious few *aides-memoires*. To love this country is to be attached, not to its past, but to its possibilities. Memory in Singapore is always oriented towards the future — projective, never retentive.

In part, this is due to our immigrant past and let us not forget, we are almost all, including a substantial number of Malay Singaporeans, descendents of immigrants. Our forefathers and mothers left things behind when they came here. Leaving things behind and setting out for the unknown is in our bones.

In part, it is due also to the circumstances of Singapore's birth as a sovereign state. Forty-five years ago, on 9 August 1965, nobody desired 9 August, for Singapore had not set out to be independent — not even Singapore's founding fathers, who had actually set out to find another country, not Singapore.

All of us came to wish for 9 August the day after on 10 August. It is difficult to see this straight, but that strange sequence, the way in which Singapore's desire for independence arose *ex post facto*, has shaped the way Singaporeans see themselves.

Because independence was not sought, we do not hark back to a founding moment. The founding moment, if it exists, exists not in the past, but rather, in that strangest tense of all, the future anterior — the tense that imagines the future as though it were already present: "You will have known what Singapore shall be when you see it." From the beginning, Singapore has always existed in the future-present.

This rare tense — common in the Romance languages — defines Singapore's self-conception. Unlike most other viable nation-states, Singapore never submits the present to the judgment of the past. Because it originated from the collapse of a prior promise — merger with Malaya — it has, from the beginning, submitted the present to the judgment of the future.

This memory of the future as the locus of hope characterises every aspect of life here. One cannot think of being Singaporean without projecting that identity into the future. The Singaporean is a being that can only exist as an ongoing, incomplete, forever half-finished project.

Similarly, one cannot see any corner of Singapore without imagining what it might look like in the future. The story of Singapore — economically and politically, materially, and spiritually — has always been oriented towards the future.

This condition is not without its costs. Ultimately, the benefits overwhelm the costs — but, still, there are costs.

The benefits: A society oriented towards the future has tremendous vitality. It tends to be open and supple, willing to absorb a wide variety of people and ideas. We remain barbarians, full of what Keynes called animal spirits. Forever a half-finished people, we are not decadent. We are primed to be members of S. Rajaratnam's "global city."

The costs: We tend to be a nation of *parvenus*. There is something of the *arriviste* in every Singaporean. A society where nostalgia is a near impossibility tends to lack refinement. We lack the stable identities that long-settled societies possess. We cannot be a nation after only 45 years, as Minister Mentor Lee Kuan Yew characteristically observed the other day. We are not Little Gidding, a comfortable and comforting village.

"If you came this way, taking the route you would be likely to take from the place you would be likely to come from..." — you will not find a familiar home.

Allow me at this point to advance two propositions that may help explain, among other things, the current controversy over the number of foreigners in our midst that Deputy Prime Minister Wong Kan Seng and others have addressed at this conference:

Proposition One: Socially meaningful life exists locally, in a particular time and place, or it does not exist at all.

Nobody can be directly acquainted with society in the mass. Someone living in Los Angeles, say, has no direct contact with something called American society. What that person has is a direct knowledge of his or her own family, circle of friends, colleagues in the workplace, and so on. This is not to deny that something called American society — or Chinese or Indian society, for that matter — has any reality. Far from it, Societies, nations, obviously act. Through the agency of the state, they go to war, make laws, administer justice, provide social safety nets and determine the socio-economic life of countless people.

But there are different levels of immediacy governing our existence as social beings. We tend to forget this when we read, say, a newspaper. By virtue of its ability to place events from different locations (Afghanistan, Shanghai, Washington, Jakarta, etc) on the uniform surface of a page, newspapers (like the rest of the media) foster the impression that all these geographically separated events can exist in a common mental space, as Ben Anderson observed once. That space does indeed exist, but the immediacy of its reality is in inverse proportion to its distance from the directly experienced facts of daily life, in particular local communities.

Proposition Two: The global economy is a fact completely at variance with the first proposition.

The global economy doubtless exists, but it has no location. It is a vast transactional system involving people who are far more unlikely to meet each other than are people who live in the same country, and are far less likely to understand each other when they do meet. If the first stage of industrialisation involved the reduction of all value to exchange value, the latest stage of capitalism involves the reduction of all communities to the status of symbols circulating in a space without location. The global economy, in other words, is everywhere and nowhere.

The problem here is how do we connect the first mode of social existence — here and now, in particular communities, in particular spaces — with that other, equally real mode, the global, which in essence has no location?

The solution obviously cannot involve shutting off the local from the global. That would be the route to economic suicide. But neither can the solution involve suppressing the local in favour of the global. There is no society that answers to a global "we"; there is no meaningful social life unless a group of people can say "we" — as in "we, the citizens of Singapore…"; and that is only possible in local communities.

Singapore and the United States are vastly different societies, but they wrestle with the same contradiction — that between the local and the global. It would be instructive to compare their experiences.

Take a look at the recent congressional elections in the US — or the 2008 presidential election, or 2004, or 2000. There is a "blue" America — Democratic — and there is a "red" America — Republican. The terms "blue" and "red" derive from the colours that CNN uses to designate Democratic and Republican states in the US presidential race. If you used those colours to designate Democratic and Republican areas down to the county level, you would see how geographically limited the Democrats are. California, for instance, a reliably Democratic state in national polls, is blue only along its densely populated coast. Apart from this sliver of land, the rest of the state is as red as the reddest of red states, like Alabama or Mississippi.

The same is true of New York and all the other states on the Eastern seaboard — blue only along their densely populated urban areas but Alabama otherwise. A US map showing how each county in each state voted would reveal a sea of red interrupted by only splashes of blue along the Pacific and Atlantic Oceans, the Gulf of Mexico, the Great Lakes, and the Mississippi and other rivers. As one commentator put it once, Democrats tend to be water people while Republicans tend to be land people.

Who are these watery people and what are the places they occupy like? The people are disproportionately young, secular, racially mixed; they are Davos people, people who would be comfortable in global milieus like the annual *World Economic Forum* in Davos. The cities — New York, San Francisco, Boston, Los Angeles — are cosmopolitan, globally connected service economies. The families with children, the churchgoers, have moved inland — the suburbs, exurbs, and rural towns of the interior. There are two Americas — one fluid, connected to global networks; and the other stolid, encased in insular communities — each marching (or not marching, as the case may be) to the beat of a different drummer.

The stolid, red America believes the fluid, blue America is rootless, feckless and un-American; and the blue America believes the red America is intolerant and anti-secular — in a word, redneck. Both views are certainly exaggerations. For example, people who distrust the cosmopolitan cultures of the coasts are not all hicks and bigots. What most of them are seeking is the shelter of stable communities, rooted in family and faith. But still the divisions continue and grow worse. Each America has a different culture, a different political party, even a different 24-hour cable news channel — Fox for the rednecks and CNN or MSNBC for the water-people.

The same thing cannot happen here? Well, the divisions here are not as pronounced yet. For one thing, it is not possible to be far from water anywhere in Singapore. Toa Payoh or Bishan are not Utah or Alabama. The cosmopolitans live in the heartland; and the heartlanders work in the cosmopolitan areas. We are so small, we cannot run away from one another. Even the most insular among us can neither avoid the world nor has any wish to do so. I doubt if there are many Sarah Palins in Singapore, with no passports. We can all swim then.

For another, politically and ideologically, we are more of a mixed bag. Consider the question of immigration — of foreign talent, etc. In America, the pro-immigrant party is the more liberal party, the Democratic Party. The iconic figure on immigration was that liberal lion, Ted Kennedy. In Singapore, the pro-immigration party is the more conservative party (at least on social and cultural issues), the People's Action Party. The iconic figure on immigration is Minister Mentor Lee Kuan Yew — a lion, but most assuredly, not a liberal. Strangely enough, it is the liberals in Singapore — at least as represented in the alternative media on the Internet and some of the speakers we have heard at this conference — who have adopted the anti-immigrant position. Such ideological confusion is sometimes productive: It helps prevent sharp divisions.

Still, it does not mean these divisions cannot arise. We have no alternative but to grapple with the contradiction at the heart of globalisation — the fact that socially meaningful life can only exist locally, here and now, but the global economy has no location and is therefore essentially rootless. We cannot solve this contradiction by abandoning one or the other side of the contradiction. We cannot shut ourselves from the world, for we would die; and we cannot abandon the local, for there is no country for rootless people.

What can we do? I think there is no alternative but to continue welcoming people from all corners of the world — and make them one of us. But we will have to better manage the process; these sudden spikes in immigrant numbers can obviously overwhelm the absorptive capacity of society. And finally, the elite in Singapore — and the Government — must continue to look out for the least among us. If the division between your globally-connected cosmopolitan elite and your locally-restricted grassroots comes to coincide dramatically with a sharp income and wealth gap, then Singapore is finished.

If you come this way, taking the route you would be likely to take from the place you would be likely to come from, then you must be able to find a more or less familiar community, a recognisable "we."

DISCUSSANT NOTES

LAI AH ENG
Panel on the Singapore Spirit

INTRODUCTION

This paper seeks to discuss our shared experiences and values, commitment to nation, and our common dreams and aspirations that shape the "Singapore Spirit." In doing so, we ask and are asked many questions about several aspects of our lives: How to build, enhance, foster, strengthen, refine, and deepen our sense of belonging, rootedness, place, heritage, history, local-global connections, engagement and involvement, local and national structures, and community ties. As commentator, I will also point out some **"how not to"** in the development and sustenance of this spirit.

SOME COMMENTS ON SPEAKERS' POINTS

The three speakers — Dr Ori Sasson, Dr Woffles Wu, and Mr Janadas Devan — have elaborated on their experiences and observations of living and engaging themselves in Singapore, and pointed out some features, strengths, and limitations of the "Singapore Spirit." Collectively, they show how — irrespective of whether they have lived in Singapore for only a relative short period as a new citizen, or for years as a citizen born and bred in Singapore — they have developed and imbibed a particular sense of this spirit which has made them feel a sense of pride and belonging to a place that is at once multi-cultural, open and forward-looking. But like many living in a fast-changing and fast-paced place, they have also expressed how Singapore generates certain ambiguities and reservations about what it is becoming and where it is headed.

KIASU-ISM: A NEGATIVE ASPECT OF THE SINGAPORE SPIRIT

Dr Ori Sasson, a "new" citizen, who has worked in Singapore for some time, observed the strength and positivity of state and national narratives, with their forward-looking messages of resilience and pragmatism, and their ideals of world-class excellence for Singapore and Singaporeans. Yet, he cannot help but notice the lack of people's narratives, and emergence of the *kiasu* (afraid to lose) attitude. I will address the lack of people's narratives later when I discuss the local community and civil society. Here, I would like to develop his point about kiasuism. I, too, have noticed this phenomenon, which seems particularly strong in some parenting cultures and even in some school cultures. Furthermore, I have noticed that some Singaporeans proudly claim *kiasuism* as a mark of being Singaporean, thus legitimating it further as a socially acceptable attitude and form of behaviour. This is a far cry from the fighting spirit of *boh kiasi* (not afraid to die) and *ai pak chia aye ia* (you have got to fight to win) common among our forefathers in Singapore's earlier days of hard work and hardship. We must not allow *kiasuism* to become an entrenched part of the "Singapore Spirit" — this attitude will make us overtly cautious and fearful of risk-taking; it would also stifle our creativity in taking initiatives and render us uncreative, unhelpful and uncaring. *Kiasuism* will only hold us back.

POSITIVE ASPECTS OF THE SINGAPORE SPIRIT

Dr Woffles Wu is appreciative of the long way Singapore has come, and the huge achievements our nation has made in meeting the basic needs of our people and in developing the infrastructure. He argues convincingly for the development of Singapore's softscape, towards the building of a vibrant city's soul, and also describes how his pursuit of excellence in his profession has contributed to his sense of belonging and to his sense of the "Singapore Spirit." His positive messages about the "Singapore Spirit" — never say die, dare to dream, out to achieve, aim to excel — is an apt reminder not to be a kiasu. His own story, and the example of the dropout-made-good that he cited, are inspiring and attest to the possibilities that the "Singapore Spirit" can bring.

MIGRATION AND THE LOCAL-GLOBAL CHALLENGE TO THE SINGAPORE SPIRIT

Mr Janadas Devan argues that meaningful life exists only or largely locally because of its immediacy, and that globalism is at variance with localism. To him, "forward-looking" Singapore, with its love of the future and not the past, seems to be rapidly eradicating and losing its localism and heading towards an economic globalism that reduces communities to symbols circulating in space without location. The challenge is not to suppress the local in favour of the global, or vice-versa, but how to be local-Singaporean and worldly-cosmopolitan at the same time. Herein lies the difficulty. Current controversies over immigration illustrate this difficulty very well, and he thinks that the pro-immigration government (versus anti-immigration "liberals") ought to manage immigration policies better, not only in the interests of localism, but also because of growing income inequality.

The theme of migration and settlement is significant and has been raised by all speakers. Here, I share my observations as a first-generation immigrant, although my stay in Singapore of almost 30 years has made me a not-so-new citizen. I have adapted to the place I once thought of as "so Chinese" when I first arrived here from Malaysia.

Singapore, of course, has a Chinese-majority population (and I am of the Hainanese minority dialect group). But its diversity and multi-culturalism is equally striking and attractive to Dr Sasson and myself, as well as to Dr Woffles Wu (who is a second- or third-generation Singaporean), and to Mr Janadas Devan (who has Malaccan Chitty Peranakan and Indian Kerala heritages).

In other words, we as Singaporeans embody and appreciate the "Singapore Spirit" of being diverse, multi-cultural, adaptive and open, given our historical and cultural origins. At the same time, Janadas and I recognise the tensions caused by immigration, in today's context of intense competition and a more settled citizenry.

While migration is a worldwide phenomenon, Singapore as a site of now huge immigration flows, mainly from Malaysia, China, and India, faces many issues of immigrant adaptation and local-migrant integration.

Settlement and adaptation are long-term processes, and both locals and immigrants need to understand that they have roles, rights and responsibilities, and that they all need to change along the way.

Both sides, for example, need to understand and recognise the generational dimensions of immigrant settlement and adaptation — the first, second, and subsequent generations will have a different sense of place, belonging and identity. Here, speaking as an immigrant of Chinese–Malaysian origin who became a citizen only after 20 years, I think the following approaches will help immigrants settle and adapt better.

Chinese immigrants from China should adjust to Chinese Singaporeans' cultural heterogeneity and not expect Chinese homogeneity, as Singapore is not a "Chinese" place despite having a Chinese — majority population. Chinese immigrants from Malaysia should not have a racialist frame of mind when encountering Malays in Singapore, as Malays here and Malays in Malaysia are different.

I share Mr Janadas Devan's call for better management of immigration policies. The government should reconsider the speed and scale of immigration, as well as the target of a population numbering six million to seven million. These policies and goals impact our range of opportunities and indeed the space available to us on this tiny island.

We also need to re-examine our policy of attracting young foreign students to study in our schools. Instead of expending large amounts of resources on them and depending on the hope that some of them will stay on to work and live in Singapore, we would do better to focus on further improving local youth's educational performance and opportunities.

MORE ON THE SINGAPORE SPIRIT

Now, I would also like to contribute to the discussion on the ongoing creation and everyday living of the "Singapore Spirit," drawing examples and insights from my findings and observations as a researcher and social anthropologist, as well as from my social activism and volunteerism. I will also draw from the shared experiences of my generation, born in the 1950s.

Multi-culturalism

My research work, findings and observations over the last 25 years have focused on the often overlapping themes of multi-culturalism, community, and identity — themes which the speakers have also raised.

I share the speakers' celebratory and positive views of Singapore's multi-culturalism, in terms of its cultural diversity and hybridity. One core area of my work is multi-culturalism at the local level, and my research shows how a historical, cultural, and symbolic map can be drawn of any local community (such as Marine Parade, which I studied). There are various meaningful individual and group activities, relationships, events and incidents taking place in such a community, in everyday life and over time. This is what gives a local community its structure, essence, and distinctiveness. These elements provide content for a community's cultural dimensions and account for the diversity and hybridity that form Singapore's particular brand of local multi-culturalism.

Much has been said and written about Singapore's official multi-culturalism, whose scope and boundaries are clearly defined by the state within the Chinese, Malay, Indian, and Others (CMIO) framework. Less is known about multi-culturalism as a ground-up phenomenon, as experienced and enacted by the country's citizens.

My research shows how dimensions of inter-ethnic and other social relations and practices are developed among residents living side-by-side and sharing common spaces. It reveals that the everyday contexts and spaces of interaction — such as the local *kopitiam*, hawker centre and other open public spaces — are potent sites which tell a complex story of deeper structures of inter-ethnic tolerance, conviviality, mutual respect and learning, as well as tensions, prejudices, and frustrations.

My research also shows how living in close proximity over time has turned public-housing residents into more collective communities, as they forge their own sense of place, learn how to better respect, tolerate and negotiate ethno-cultural differences, and how to negotiate with one another and with authorities with regards to their needs and desires.

My general conclusion is that the agency of ordinary citizens actively shapes Singapore's continuous evolving multi-culturalism (and here, there is no lack of the "people's narratives," as pointed out by Dr Sasson). This multi-culturalism both arises from and flourishes despite a state-planned environment and may coincide or collide with state multi-culturalism. As part of the "Singapore Spirit," ground-up multi-culturalism as everyday lived reality, ideal, value, process and practice is natural and spontaneous, rooted in the actions of ordinary citizens.

Many academics and observers are critical of the official CMIO multi-racial framework. They also think that there is, at best, tolerance — but that this is not good enough. I share their criticism of the rigidity of the CMIO ethnic categories and how these lead to divisive tendencies and ethnicised views and stereotypes.

I also agree that tolerance is not enough. But it is a minimum condition and value that every society must possess, and which Singapore does possess. Tolerance needs to be appreciated in its particular form, context, strength, and spirit. It is also important to recognise that familiarity, civility, tolerance, respect, appreciation, building of common ground, and ability to negotiate differences and tensions, particularly at the local level, were gradually built and honed over several decades. These values and skills constitute a priceless social and cultural capital, notwithstanding the challenges generated by ethno-centrism and the occasional incident of racial tension.

Top-down multiculturalism alone cannot work. The challenge now is to nurture, develop and transfer this social-cultural capital, over and over again, to every child, every generation, and every local community, at a time and in a context of rapid change, intense competition, individualism, and a growing inequality that partially overlaps with ethnicity.

Local community

My work has also explored the meanings of living and senses of place and belonging in the Housing and Development Board (HDB) heartlands. Because 85% of Singaporeans are HDB residents, these are dimensions of everyday and social significance in Singapore life. I pose the following broad questions in the context of strong state intervention and growing social diversity and differences:

- How can the policy-maker, the policy-informer, the planner and the researcher be firmly grounded in social realities and needs while formulating policies and making recommendations, so that the process is not top-down but rather informed and inclusive?

- How can they, and we, not let market or political-bureaucratic forces dictate and dominate views and decisions about local communities?

I do not question the qualifications and intentions of professionals. I am referring to the public–private housing divide that has come to characterise Singapore's class differences. In this context, public-housing residents are commonly viewed as homogeneous *hoi polloi* "heartlanders" who live in "pigeonholes" in uniform and non-aesthetic high-rise blocks of flats in somewhat "unauthentic" communities, in contrast to sophisticated "cosmopolitans" who live in beautiful designer homes in condominiums, semi-detached houses and bungalows in posh districts.

This housing/class divide has led to the "othering" of HDB-dwellers — an unconscious tendency I have observed in some Singaporeans, including professionals who are policy-makers, planners, and decision-makers. This "othering" leads some to think that HDB dwellers will ask a mile if given an inch, that they will "abuse the system," that they have no sense of aesthetics, and that they do not know what they want or what is good for them.

It is a view, attitude, and bias that excludes, not includes. I also think that within this divide, this category of policy-makers, planners, and decision-makers contradict themselves. On the one hand, they provide public housing and promote a sense of community; on the other, they seem to let bureaucratic, market and even political forces prevail over a sense of place, belonging and community.

Several examples come to mind: The growing corporatisation of the public, social, and community institutions — wet markets, hawker centres, and *kopitiams* — that exist in the local community; pricing that makes public housing and home-ownership increasingly unaffordable; and the drawing and re-drawing of the boundaries of political wards, with scant respect for a sense of place and belonging, let alone geography. (I once took my children to visit a friend in Serangoon and when we arrived, my daughter said: "But we are still in Marine Parade.")

A final example comes from my observations as a residents' representative in my HDB precinct's main upgrading programme committee. The planners wanted to cut down the trees in the open-air car park and build a "modern" multi-storey one. We representatives had to negotiate very hard with the architects and planners over design, layout, facilities, and materials, but the hardest battle was fighting against that five-storey icon of HDB modernity, for reasons of cost, security, ventilation and cleanliness. Guess who won?

Civil society

From my experiences as an activist, I wish to make a point about how to and how not to participate in civil society.

Most of us are aware of the "AWARE saga" which took place in 2009. Briefly, a group of women, under the urgings of a self-declared "feminist mentor" and through instant mass-membership voting and a constitutional loophole, got themselves elected onto the central committee of the 24-year-old women's organisation the Association of Women for Action and Research (AWARE).

As a founding and life member of AWARE, I have witnessed its contributions to Singapore's and women's development and interests over the years, and thus found myself having to rise to the occasion in order to reclaim the association.

The seven-hour-long and rather cacophonous *Extraordinary General Meeting* through which this group of women was finally ousted was not — contrary to common perception — "petty politics" or a women's "catfight" internal to the organisation. At heart were many issues and values all worth "fighting" about and for: Leadership, governance, transparency, consultation, civility, ethics, inclusivity, trust, rights, imagination, conviction, democratic participation and rules of engagement, the issues and quality of debate, volunteerism, sexuality, conservatism, liberalism, religion, and state intervention.

The AWARE saga of 2009 is an important event in the history of civil society and public life in Singapore. AWARE was formed in 1985 as one of the first civil-society organisations, at a time of strong state and social authoritarianism. The association was guided by what it thought was right, fair, and good. It did not obey the traditional authoritarian "shut up and sit down" principle but built up the "stand up and speak out" spirit. In doing so, AWARE made many contributions to Singapore women and society. By clearly rejecting unacceptable ethics and practices, the AWARE saga showed that this spirit was alive and kicking. The passion, conviction and courage with which AWARE members fought for what is right, fair and good portend well. The greatest gain from the AWARE saga for women, civil society and Singapore is this spirit: Not to shut up and sit down but to stand up and speak out.

Inequality, class reproduction, meritocracy, competition and compassion

My final point, drawn from the shared experiences of my generation, is about social inequality and social mobility and how the "Singapore Spirit" can deal with these issues.

As someone born in the mid-1950s and educated during the 1960s and 1970s, I have witnessed and benefited from the "Third World to First World" experience that Singapore and some other countries went through. For some members of my generation, it meant a great leap from poverty to plenty, from working class to middle class, from backwardness to modernity, from mediocrity to excellence.

This was a great and unprecedented leap for us and our families, with barely educated or illiterate parents. We were the first in our poor families to obtain higher education. But the context is now fast changing. Income inequality is increasing. Mobility through meritocracy is getting more limited as class reproduction takes place, in which the upwardly mobile and well-to-do ensure the economic and social mobility of their children through education, employment and other opportunities, advantages, and privileges. What does this class reproduction through economic and social mobility do and mean for the "Singapore Spirit"?

There is nothing wrong with seeking economic and social mobility. It is the right thing to do — to get out of poverty and attain a decent standard of living. But class reproduction of the upwardly mobile and well-to-do, with their better resources, can lead to inequality as the playing field becomes increasingly uneven while those lacking in resources are left behind and out-competed.

The principles of meritocracy and equality — so strongly upheld in the spirit of Singapore — are not yet dead. But they are no longer as strongly operative as they were during the formative years of my generation. The issue of mobility needs to be addressed with urgency before growing income and other attendant inequalities get worse. How can wealth and other resources be better distributed in order to assure meritocratic mobility in the face of class reproduction and intense educational and economic competition?

As education is the main vehicle for economic and social mobility for the vast majority of Singaporeans, how can we ensure that children from less well-to-do, poor and disadvantaged backgrounds get fair chances in good education at all levels? And in the spirit of Singapore, how can we inculcate a spirit of compassion, rather than competition, among our youths? For example, can well-to-do children who do well academically and receive government scholarships be encouraged to put their scholarship monies into funds for their less-endowed fellow students? (My daughter tried to do so through the Ministry of Education's scholarship scheme, but there is currently no such system in place). Compassion and competition are not inconsistent or conflicting values; on the contrary, they make a powerful combination for a win-win situation.

CONCLUSION

The "Singapore Spirit" means many things to many people. I think that it is deeply rooted in our histories and experiences of migration and settlement over several generations and in our everyday cultures of living to be humble, fair, civil, tolerant, open, inclusive, and compassionate, as well as hard-working and enterprising. With these values, we can look forward to resolving our internal problems and facing globalisation with a deep sense of place and belonging, and with confidence and creativity.

Postscript: The commentator notes that some of the issues she has raised — the policies and top-down attitudes of policy- and decision-makers towards citizens and HDB dwellers, immigration policies, inequalities and class reproduction — were key issues raised in the General Election of 7 May 2011 and identified as some of the main causes for the ruling party losing some Parliamentary seats to the opposition. She hopes that the promise of rethink and reform will be sustained, applied to major public policies affecting economic, political, and social life, and that all stakeholders will be involved in a democratic and consultative manner. She attributes this political springtime to the spirit of Singapore.

SECTION V

Special Session

CHAPTER 10

People's Association: Co-creating a Great Home and Caring Community

LIM BOON HENG

Thank you for inviting me to share with you the work of the People's Association (PA) and its GrasRroots Organisations (GROs) with regards to building social capital in Singapore.

The PA turned 50 last year. Its fundamental role of promoting racial harmony and fostering social cohesion in Singapore has not changed, although the mission statement — "To build and bridge communities to achieve One People, One Singapore" — was refreshed recently.

The Singapore of the past is very different from the Singapore of today. Attracting people to a community centre or club used to be very much easier. In the 1960s, all that was needed was setting up a black-and-white TV set, and the *kampong* folks would flock to the Community Centre (CC). As the two existing channels broadcast in English and Malay, and Chinese and Tamil respectively, Singaporeans watched most programmes in common, strengthening the message that we are a multi-racial society. No one has done a sociological study as far as I know, so we do not know how watching common programmes broke down racial barriers. As most people lived in the same neighbourhood for a long time, the opportunities for coming together at CCs helped to strengthen mutual trust and deepen bonds of friendship.

Thirty years ago, when I was first elected to Parliament, the Residents' Committees (RCs) were newly formed. Singaporeans were being uprooted from the *kampongs* and settled into Housing and Development Board (HDB) new towns. Old ties were disrupted. RCs were set up to build new communities. Block parties' organised by RCs were a novelty and attracted many residents. Children's parties, in particular, were a hit, and initially a sure way of bringing parents from different families together. Over time, however, the parents felt more secure about leaving their children with the RC members, and they stayed home to do housework instead! This challenged RC members to come up with new activities to attract residents.

As a rookie Member of Parliament (MP) in the 1980s, I was grateful for the advice that seasoned MPs gave. I remember what the late Mr Fong Sip Chee said to some of us: "You must remember what grassroots events are for. These events are not held for their own sake, but in order to bring people together, so that they can become friends and good neighbours. And at these functions, you should take the opportunity to address issues of the day, and explain policies."

The world has changed. The speakers before me spoke about the challenges of a global city, of an ageing population, of how rapid growth and developments such as the influx of foreign talent has brought about increasing disparities and created divides. They spoke about the need to strike a balance between globalisation and maintaining our local identity, about the need to nurture a caring society, and the need to build the Singapore spirit, with shared values and experiences, a commitment to the nation, and the common dreams and aspirations of citizens.

Indeed, the CCs and RCs have also evolved to meet the changing needs and aspirations of residents. CCs have evolved both in terms of offerings and in terms of infrastructure. Sports popular in the 1960s, such as boxing and weight-lifting, have been replaced by *tai chi, taekwondo* and yoga. Art classes for children, cooking, cake-making, Japanese language classes and flower arrangement were the most popular courses during the 1980s, and drew many residents to the CCs. Then, in the 1990s, the most popular courses became aerobics, international folk dance, choral singing, ballet and piano. Language and culinary classes have continued to be popular.

As the demand for and needs of CC courses changed, so has the infrastructure. In the 1990s, the CCs began to co-locate with major community agencies such as libraries, neighbourhood police posts, post offices, and polyclinics. In recent times, CCs co-locate with swimming pools and other sports facilities. These changes reflect the struggle of the grassroots organisations to bring people together, as more attention is given to multiple TV channels and the Internet in their own homes, or attractions elsewhere. It is a struggle against social drift, as described by Robert Putnam's book *Bowling Alone*.

Slowly, the attention of grassroots leaders turned to activities that would attract residents. The focus turned to the activities themselves, and GROs developed an over-reliance on lucky draws. While the numbers of attendees at grassroots activities stayed high, MPs observed that they tended to see the same familiar faces at these events.

When I was appointed PA Deputy Chairman in 2007, I looked at the performance, and, frankly, saw more output than outcome. Grassroots leaders and PA staff were all working extremely hard. But were we satisfied with the outcome? How well were we progressing in developing our common identity and sense of belonging, against the social forces at work? Should we attempt a review of PA and the work of GROs under its umbrella? We took the plunge, and went through a two-year exercise involving the PA Board, the Ministry of Community Development, Youth and Sports, advisors and grassroots representatives.

The result was the co-creation of one common vision for the community, that of "A Great Home and A Caring Community where we share our values, pursue our passions, fulfill our hopes, and treasure our memories." Our vision tagline is "Our Community, My Responsibility."

With this common vision, we asked grassroots leaders to envision what they wanted their community to be in five years' time, and to do their work-plans so that each year's efforts would contribute towards that community. In other words, all their efforts should lead to the accumulation of social capital. This they have done — their efforts have been compiled in the publication *Community 2015 Master Plan and Work Plan*.

The key components of social capital are: Trust and reciprocity between people, informal networks, and confidence in the government and public institutions. Robert Putnam's definition of social capital brought back to my mind the advice of the late Mr Fong Sip Chee. He defined the work of

MPs and their grassroots leaders in his own way that they add up to accumulating social capital!

In this light, the role of grassroots leaders is not that of event organisers, but that of community facilitators. High social capital must involve most, if not all residents, and not a minority. So how do grassroots leaders get more residents to participate, to take ownership? Getting thousands of residents to attend an event is not difficult, but when they come, do they participate and interact? There is more interaction and deeper engagement when people gather in small groups. When the group is large, many become passive attendees. When groups are small, everybody plays their part. Likewise, grassroots leaders observe a greater sense of ownership when residents organise pot-luck floor parties, compared to the block parties organised by the RCs.

Here, we can learn from what other organisations have done: Give everyone a role. When there is a sense of ownership, there is a sense of belonging. Both small- and large-scale events contribute to building social capital.. For example, large-scale events like the *National Day Parade* can allow people to participate in groups where they identify with one another. Large-scale events, like when Singapore wins a trophy in a sports competition, also give everyone a common high and a sense of common identity. But large-scale events must be complemented by many small-scale ones, such as interest groups.

How do we know when grassroots leaders have succeeded? When small interest groups are self-sustaining, and do not rely on the RCs or Community Club Management Committee (CCMC) to organise activities for them. When residents become good friends and look out for one another in what Dr Maliki calls "micro-communities," like when a nurse and a taxi-driver become community resources to help a diabetic neighbour improve his quality of life.

Local problems are solved by residents when they step forward and work with one another. For instance, when some people who make use of the HDB void deck become a nuisance, the block residents get together to regulate things and make sure they do not make noise at odd hours. These are scenarios that we will see, when our grassroots leaders, as Community Facilitators, put the resident — not the activity — at the centre of what they do.

There will be no end to this work. There will be changes in society, such as the influx of new immigrants, as we have witnessed in recent years, and each new decade will bring new issues and challenges. Some old trends, however, will continue too, such as the frequency with which Singaporeans change homes, at least in the immediate and medium-term future. And we must never take racial and religious harmony for granted.

There is a renewed sense of purpose among grassroots leaders today. They know what their role is: To harness their residents in a common effort to co-create "A Great Home and a Caring Community." There is also a new buzz and sense of excitement among the PA staff, as they now see their role clearly: To support grassroots leaders in bridging divides and communities, to forge a common identity and help us all become more rooted to this, our home.

11

Mercy Relief: Adding Gloss to the Gifted Dot

HASSAN AHMAD

ENVIED BUT LOVED?

While Singapore as a country is envied for her economic achievements, are we Singaporeans loved as a nation by our neighbours?

Singapore is a naturally gifted dot — geographically well-positioned for commerce, and safe from many calamities. Such blessings become valuable only if they are shared by Singaporeans who pay it forward to fulfill our humanitarian responsibilities.

When a disaster occurs in the region, it is as much a test for our neighbours as it is for us. Are we mere fair-weather friends or passive bystanders to the sufferings of others? Or do we take the initiative in helping to relieve our neighbours' pains?

Compassionate hearts make for a respectable and desirable nation, where kindness is the true basis of faith that fuses the people. Ultimately, if we can care for the strangers around us, then caring will no longer be strange among us and within us.

Figure 1 Binding faiths — Leaders of various faiths from Singapore participating in the 100th Day memorial of the 2004 tsunami at the Ground Zero in Banda Aceh, reflecting the spirit of humanity regardless of country, culture, or creed.

NEIGHBOURS' VIEWS AND THE REALITY

I would like to share the views of two well-known regional social powerhouses, whom I met in the course of my humanitarian work.

- Mr Mechai Viravaidya, Chairman and founder of the Population and Community Development Association, the largest non-governmental organisation (NGO) in Thailand, with 600 staff and 12,000 volunteers. He is also the former Thai Deputy Minister for Industry.

  "Singapore should share some of its wealth and development success with its neighbours to help improve the lives of needy communities in the region."

- H.E. Surin Pitsuwan, Secretary-General of the Association of Southeast Asian Nations (ASEAN). He is the former Thai Foreign Minister, who visited Mercy Relief (MR) in Singapore in 2004.

  "Having proven her mettle in the economic sector globally, Singapore/Singaporeans should do more in the region to project the 'Heart of the Lion'."

SINGAPORE SPIRIT EXTENDS ACROSS THE REGION

As members of a global community, Singaporeans have already become increasingly conscious that the "Singapore Spirit" is about more than just our own development and progress. It is also about our ability to extend a spirit of compassion beyond our own borders — addressing the needs of others, and, in tandem, addressing the question of what makes life meaningful for us.

Through MR alone, tens of thousands of Singaporeans have stepped forward as regional citizens, sacrificing their time, energy, and comfort, and at times even risking their personal safety to reach out to the disadvantaged in the region. MR has seen many Singaporeans volunteering to participate in overseas relief and development work, and many others who have directly supported these overseas operations by raising funds, sorting and packing relief supplies, and garnering and activating other volunteers. There are also amazing individuals and corporations who repeatedly write cheques to ensure that members of relief operations do not worry about financial resources.

Figure 2 Next generation extends compassion — Children in Singapore, joined by MR Goodwill Ambassador Stefanie Sun, penned notes of encouragement and hope to their foreign counterparts affected by the 2008 Wenchuan earthquake.

Here are some examples of the thousands who have come forward:

- Kudos to the doctors and nurses (both general surgeons and specialists), and pharmacists from the Singhealth Group, National Healthcare Group and Parkway Healthcare Group for supporting their personnel by granting them with unrecorded leave when they go for overseas medical relief missions.

- The paramedics from the Singapore Civil Defence Force (SCDF) have played key roles during post-disaster emergency relief phases.
- Logistic specialists such as those from the Neptune Orient Lines (NOL) coordinated the shipment of containers to Aceh and personally decorated those containers for use as kindergartens to help restore normalcy in Aceh after the 2004 tsunami.
- Architects like Associate Profesor Tay Kheng Soon of Akitek Tenggara and the National University of Singapore also chipped in, not only with his time and expertise, but with a substantial sum of his own money for tsunami reconstruction projects in Meulaboh, Aceh.
- In the immediate aftermath of the 2004 tsunami, professional SilkAir pilots and the Chief Executive officer (CEO) of an international Public Relations (PR) firm swopped their ties for their T-shirts and helped clear the mountains of debris in Meulaboh, to pave the way for reconstruction works.
- Students from Singapore Polytechnic (SP) went to Padang in 2009 after the massive earthquake there. SP's Civil Defence Lionhearters Club sacrificed their school holidays to help unpack, sort and repack more than 20 truckloads of food and household items donated by the Carrefour International Foundation to distribute to the victims.
- Celebrities like MR's Goodwill ambassadors Stefanie Sun and Hady Mirza took time off to help attend to the "heartware" of the beneficiaries while MR provided the hardware after the Asian tsunami, the Wenchuan and Padang earthquakes;
- Religious institutions from the major faiths contributed substantially, in terms of volunteers and donations, for most major disasters. Institutions like the Singapore Soka Association (SSA), Majlis Ugama Islam Singapura (MUIS) and the Catholic Archdiocese, have contributed substantially to the humanitarian cause.
- Thousands of Singaporean children helped put together Play Packs and wrote notes of consolation and encouragement to their peers overseas who were overwhelmed by the fury of nature.

- SCDF officers sacrificed their own annual leave to train slum communities in North Sumatera in fire safety and drills, as part of a disaster risk mitigation effort.

Back in Singapore, thousands have selflessly braved our tropical heat to raise funds for sustaining relief operations; and sorted and packed relief supplies for dispatch to affected locations.

- Families spent days and nights volunteering at MR's supplies centres while large corporations such as HSL Constructor and MediaCorp conducted fundraising projects to garner more donations.
- Hundreds of youths and working adults sacrificed their comfort, school holidays and annual leave to be deployed through the Mercy Overseas Volunteers Expedition (MOVE) Programme to serve at MR's project locations. To name a few:

(a) Youth leaders from SSA,
(b) Students from Madrasah Aljunied,
(c) Students from SP,
(d) Admin scholars of Alpha Society,
(e) Management trainees from the Singapore Tourism Board.

The spirit of giving and the outpouring of compassion and sacrifice by Singaporeans when given the right platforms have been real and amazing. Interestingly, some religious leaders from the various faiths opined that, apart from the sound policies of Singapore's political leaders, Singaporeans' charitable spirit has also helped keep Singapore blessed and prosperous.

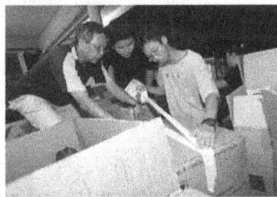

Figure 3 Charity does not end at home — Mr Teh Thien Yew and his family volunteered for a month at MR's supplies centre to help sort and pack relief items for overseas distribution to tsunami-affected communities.

SPIRIT AND PHILOSOPHY OF REGIONAL SERVICE

To accommodate Singaporeans' growing interests in serving our regional neighbours, MR has set up a structured programme called MOVE — Mercy Overseas Volunteers Expeditions. Through this programme, Singaporeans can contribute and serve at our project locations. Its slogan, "It is Good To Feel Bad," reminds our returning volunteers that it is good to feel bad about not having given enough, as there are always fellow human beings in our region who are much worse off than us in sunny and comfortable Singapore.

The philosophy of service — "He who serves others, serves himself last" — reminds us that when we serve the needs of others, we should not be thinking of what or how we are going to benefit. That should be the last thing on our minds.

So, why do Singaporeans find it more interesting or perhaps more fulfilling to go abroad to volunteer? It could be that there are more severe needs out there which require urgent attention. These require volunteers to play larger and more significant roles, compared to volunteering with the more established systems servicing the needy here in Singapore. As such, the latter may provide the volunteers with fewer opportunities to fulfill their social aspirations.

Figure 4 Novelty for nobleness — The pedal-powered iWater filtration systems, designed by Singaporean environment company Glowtec, helped overcome water issues faced by disaster-stricken communities in Taiwan, Pakistan, Philippines, Myanmar, Yemen, and Sri Lanka. The 800 litres per hour manual systems are particularly useful for affected remote areas without power supply.

MOVING FORWARD

The aim is to develop MR as a humanitarian organisation, as well as the humanitarian industry in general. In this way, Singaporeans will have more opportunities that hone the compassion within them.

Asian countries that are geographically concentrated in high-risk areas continue to be exposed to a range of natural disasters. These vulnerabilities are compounded by chronic poverty. Findings from the United Nations Intergovernmental Panel on Climate Change (IPCC) have confirmed that climate change is one of the most important challenges to the social, economic, and environmental well-being of countries in the Pacific region. According to the World Bank, Vietnam — with 3,200km of coastline — now ranks in the top five countries that will be hardest hit by climate change. The impact of climate change is already being felt by our Southeast Asian neighbours, and is expected to worsen in the coming decades.

Given our advantageous position, both geographically and economically, Singapore is well-placed to play a significant role. This will allow the "Singapore Spirit" to grow and spread across the region. Among other things, new strategic initiatives from MR include:

- Embarking on research for development of technological solutions for rural and disaster-stricken communities.
- Educating and grooming the next generation of humanitarians. We are working on this with SP, which has started running its first Diploma programme in Humanitarian Affairs.
- Sowing the seeds of compassion into the young, especially pre-schoolers and lower Primary students. We are working with Nanyang Polytechnic to develop Little Mercy Online Games.
- Continue cultivating Singaporean hearts. We are working with Community Development Councils (CDCs) and the SSA on the "Cultivating a Grateful and Gracious Society" campaigns.

Such initiatives have allowed and will allow for more Singaporeans to become acquainted with, participate in, and contribute towards the humanitarian cause, and in tandem, increase the depth and breadth of the Singaporean spirit of giving and sharing.

Singaporeans have been actively seeking reliable platforms and conduits of compassion to fulfill their social aspirations, to give and share. This sharing of love and blessings with fellow regional citizens is an essential part of our own education and development, as individuals, as a community, and as a nation.

However, there is a caveat for Singaporeans serving the needs of foreign communities — that common sense is not always common. What is commonly acceptable in our society or culture may not be so for the beneficiary communities. We cannot impose our values, beliefs or cultures, just because we are offering our help. Nonetheless, we can still endeavour to influence their mindsets and habits for the sake of their development and progress.

CONCLUSION

Should Singapore have a government-driven overseas development vehicle?

Many in the region may not know how much Singaporeans have provided for our neighbours, especially over the last couple of years. To a large extent, this is probably due to that fact that the "Singapore Spirit" — that spirit of sharing and helping others — is not adulterated by politics or commerce.

Singaporeans give because we feel we ought to give and we want to. We are happy about giving to improve the lives of the disadvantaged in our midst and bring a little cheer to them.

From 2008 to 2010 alone, MR implemented relief and reconstruction projects worth $6.3 million at 18 disaster-hit locations over ten countries. Another $3.5 million was spent on 20 sustainable development projects for poverty-stricken communities in four countries. These projects were made possible by donations from individuals, social and corporate institutions, and the government of Singapore. We are confident that this great spirit of sharing will continue to grow, and we will try to garner more New Citizens to come onboard this volunteering and philanthropic bandwagon as quickly as possible.

In view of how various countries have implemented overseas disaster relief missions and development programmes through their respective governmental humanitarian agencies such as Australian Government

Overseas Aid Program (AUSAID), Japan International Cooperation Agency (JICA) and United States Agency for International Development (USAID), one might ask: Should Singapore set up its own Singapore Agency for International Development (SINGAID)?

Despite being only seven years old, MR is already quite firmly etched in the minds of many Singaporeans as the "people's NGO." Being locally born and bred, it is proof that Singaporeans have become a caring nation of people who have the tenacity to act on their humanitarian inclinations. The growth of MR may just illustrate where the nation's interest lies — for social organisations to develop and flourish on their own, rather than under the auspices of another government-driven initiative.

Over the years, MR has seen the two faces of humanity — the dreadful side, which has brought death, pain, devastation and anguish; and the side marked by the great spirit of selflessness, volunteerism and philanthropy, which has made it an extraordinary experience for all who have extended their helping hands.

Figure 5 As the conduit of Singaporeans' compassion to the region, MR has been able to serve hundreds of thousands of distressed and disadvantaged lives yearly.

Conclusion

12

Closing Remarks: Living and Breathing "Singapore"

GILLIAN KOH

A range of important issues and a diverse set of perspectives on each of them have been discussed by both the speakers and participants at this conference that focused on fostering a more inclusive society in Singapore.

It has been said that "where you stand, will depend on where you sit." What resonates with you will be shaped by what you do, the sector you are from, and who you are. The best that I can do when trying to draw out some key conclusions to the conference is to share with you what I take away from it.

Let me begin with the context for today's conference. First, we find ourselves in a global city, and the speakers accepted that as the starting point of the discussion. Nobody disputed that. However, as speaker Mr T. Sasitharan and keynote speaker Deputy Prime Minister Wong Kan Seng have suggested, the challenge is — how do we make a global city a home?

How do we make it a place with a soul? If it were a place without a soul, then nobody would want to be here, and nobody would want to stay. Mr Sasitharan said that something to the order of a thousand people leave our shores each year. These may be the young, the talented and others we know less about.

What makes this such a challenge? First, Mr Janadas Devan talked about how our unnatural birth as an unintended nation makes this difficult. Second, the destruction of historical markers also makes it difficult to have a sense of place and identity. As one participant remarked that his father can no longer recognise Singapore when he is driven around the island. This participant added that on the other end of the generational spectrum was his son whose life revolved around the iPad. As such, the participant was trying to convey his worry that there was just not enough to root Singaporeans to their geography, to their historical legacy and certainly even less to string one generation of citizens to the next.

Third, we have the problem of economic globalisation. With it comes the negative effect of wage disparities where we see wage levels being driven down at the bottom level of the labour market. Of course, we have heard of the many policies that have been devised to mitigate that, but it is truly not an easy problem to deal with. These are the reasons it is particularly difficult to make Singapore an endearing home.

What do we do then? If there was time, I would ask you to close your eyes and imagine that you were the parent of a special-needs child, a resident of a one-room flat, someone who is an older worker, struggling to make ends meet. In such a scenario, would you feel that society was just and fair? Would you feel included, not just as part of a global city, but as part of a home?

This process of introspection or reflection that Mr Kok Heng Leun talked so profoundly is not something that you have waited to get to the theatre in order to do. It is something that you can do every day. And I think Mr Yam Ah Mee has highlighted how an organisation like the *People's Association* is constantly trying to expose us to and interact with what we think is "the other." But it is not "the other." It is our neighbour living in geographically close proximity, since Singapore is so small. Therefore, do we have any excuse for not understanding? Do we have any excuse for not "closing our eyes" to ask ourselves: What if the shoe was on the other foot?

In addition to that introspection, I was deeply impressed by Dr Woffles Wu's catalogue of the creative talent that Singapore is built on. What it means is that we are not alone. Many others have struggled before us. His stories spoke to me about the spirit of self-belief on the ground. One thing we can do, apart from the more abstract thought exercises, is to write the stories not just about, say, Minister Mentor Lee Kuan Yew — who is about to launch yet another book about his thoughts on Singapore — but complement that by compiling the personal stories of the people who have moved out of the one-room flat, the beneficiaries of Pathlight School for autistic children run by speaker Ms Denise Phua, of which I am a grateful parent of a beneficiary, the croupier cited by Mr Ong Ye Kung who has doubled her pay by working at the casino.

With that, we will better understand what makes Singapore different and special. Even if one were born in a one-room flat today, you will have a reason to nurture hope, and a basis for self-belief. Accompanying that, you will find that there are state policies, business people with a sense of corporate social responsibility, as well as civil society activists who will provide extra help so you can achieve a decent livelihood and even social mobility. So, we should allocate time towards these deep personal processes. We just need to look at who our neighbour is.

When we do that, we may find the answers to some of the questions that have not been fully addressed today. First, looking at our poor, the people who are squeezed in the middle (people who are not poor enough to be helped by current social assistance schemes and yet not rich enough to sustain their livelihoods) as cited by Mr Raja Segar, and the people who are disadvantaged — do they receive adequate help from the government, civil society, or from the businessmen who pay the daily wages to these people? These were issues raised by Ms Sylvia Lim, Dr Lai Ah Eng, and many other participants. Have we done enough to make Singapore an inclusive society for them?

Second, do we or do we not have a soul? If we have the stories, I am certain that the sense of soul will awaken. I leave it to the Heritage Board, the journalists, the artists, and literally, the grandchildren of the people who have built Singapore brick by brick, to write these stories and to share them.

Another question for which we do not yet have a good answer: Is there space for political diversity, and even political dissidents in Singapore? Mr Sasitharan told us that he has remained in Singapore, not because he believes that the country has a soul but because he is fighting to forge a soul. He said that the starting point cannot just be about what he has done or is doing, but that it must include the stories of the late opposition politician Mr J.B. Jeyaratnam, the ex-ISA detainee Ms Teo Soh Lung, and the late playwright Mr Kuo Pao Kun. That may be the frontier of how far we have to go to develop an inclusive society, by Mr Sasitharan's reckoning.

When we do that, we will also begin to understand the place of foreigners in Singapore today. According to Census 2010, 64% of the total population in Singapore is made up of citizens, but even that does not account for how many within this group are people who are locally-born, and how many are like Mr Ori Sasson — new immigrants. If we develop our sense of soul, we may better understand the human spirit that drives the foreigners here that once drove our ancestors here. It also means that we will be humble and we will find our common humanity. As Dr Wu pointed out, as we move from Third World to First, we must remind ourselves to eschew the temptation to become arrogant, condescending and *kiasu*.

So those are the tough questions that remain unanswered because they need to be answered by you, the individuals at this conference. This needs to be done through your own personal process of introspection.

Finally, what can we do? First, I would say that we should begin to welcome everyone to share their "grandfather stories," the "Tan Ah Teck" stories. Many of them deserve to be recorded and circulated. In this Internet age, we can create many portals where these can be shared and discussed. We can also include the stories that Mr Hassan Ahmad has shared with us to illustrate the generousity of the Singapore Spirit.

Second, as we arrive at the point where we understand the Singapore Spirit and celebrate it, the sense of service will follow. If we have that change in the "chambers of our hearts," as Ms Phua put it, that service will flow. As a Minister said in Parliament recently, it is very difficult to mandate a love for one's parents, and yet, this government tries. We know that that is not the solution. It begins in the heart.

When do we arrive? There is a lot of talk about the relevant key performance indicators for volunteerism, philanthropy, a caring community and the fact that we have soul. Well, the only thing I can say is that "what can be counted is not always valuable; what is valuable cannot always be counted." So, if we have arrived, we will only be able to feel it, share it, and spread it. With that, hopefully, we will become a great little nation.

About the Contributors

Hassan Ahmad, 40, was the first Executive Director of Mercy Relief (2003–2006) who has extensive field experience in the area of humanitarian relief. He has planned, coordinated, and led Singaporean civilian and medical missions to war-torn Afghanistan (2002), earthquake-hit Iran (2004) and Pakistan (2005), tsunami-battered Aceh and Sri Lanka (2004/5), floods in Yemen (2008), cyclone Nargis in Myanmar (2008), and Wenchuan earthquake (2008). Equally experienced in managing relief deployments for armed conflicts, he led and coordinated relief operations for conflict-stricken areas including Gaza, Sri Lanka, and Pakistan.

In 2006, he helped the Lien Foundation to set up its regional humanitarian arm, Lien Aid, and became its first Chief Executive, focusing on water and sanitation issues in rural areas in Asia (2006–2008). He returned to Mercy Relief in March 2008 and was appointed as Chief Executive, having completed a United Nations Office for Coordination of Humanitarian Affairs (UN OCHA) policy review with the Stockholm International Peace Research Institute (SIPRI) on the Effectiveness of Foreign Military Assets in Natural Disasters. His work was published into a book in March 2008. From 2008 to 2010, he headed various studies by Mercy Relief to produce original researched papers for contributions to UN-endorsed publications with United Nations Office for International Development Research Centre (UN IDRC), World Health Organization (WHO), United Nations Children's Fund (UNICEF), and United Nations International Strategy for Disaster reduction (UNISDR).

Under his leadership, Mercy Relief have touched the lives and hearts in more than 19 countries and successfully maintaining the 72-hour emergency response time. In 2008, he expanded Mercy Relief's scope from mainly emergency relief to include sustainable development programme for disadvantaged communities and initiated *strategic initiatives* which include *inter alia* embarking on *research for development* of technological solutions for rural and disaster-stricken communities, the introduction of courses in humanitarian affair to train and groom future aid workers.

A road warrior who firmly believes that the world's future hinges on the proper management of the progress of rural communities, Hassan enliven his humanitarian commitment by serving with passion on the adamantine that *He Who Serves Others Serves Himself Last.*

Derek da CUNHA is an independent scholar. He is the author of *Singapore Places its Bets: Casinos, Foreign Talent and Remaking a City-state* (pp. 192, 2010). His other single-authored work is the book *The Price of Victory: The 1997 Singapore General Election and Beyond* (1997). He is also the editor of the volumes *Debating Singapore: Reflective Essays* (1994), and *Singapore in the New Millennium: Challenges Facing the City-State* (2002). He has MPhil and PhD degrees in the field of international relations from Cambridge University and the Australian National University respectively. Dr da Cunha's research interests are eclectic. Beyond political and social commentary, he has also written extensively on defence and security issues. He is currently working on two books: One on a socio-political theme, and another related to an appraisal of the evolving geopolitical situation in Southeast Asia.

Faizal bin Yahya is a Research Fellow with the Institute of Policy Studies (IPS), Lee Kuan Yew School of Public Policy (LKYSPP) at the National University of Singapore (NUS). Prior to his current appointment he was an Assistant Professor in the South Asian Studies Programme, Faculty of Arts and Social Sciences at NUS. He was also a Visiting Research Fellow, Institute of Southeast Asian Studies (ISEAS), Singapore from January 2008 to June 2009. He was conferred his PhD from the University of Sydney, Australia in 2000. His latest co-authored book with Ms Arunajeet Kaur is entitled; *The Migration of Indian Human Capital, to Southeast Asia* by Routledge published in November 2010. He has written more than 20 journal articles and book chapters. His other two books are *Economic Cooperation between Singapore and India: An Alliance in the Making?*, Routledge, United Kingdom, 2008 and *New "Temples" of India: Singapore and India Collaboration in Information Technology Parks*, Social Sciences in Asia, Brill, Leiden and Boston, 2008. He is in the Economics and Business cluster and his current research interests include transnationals, human and social capital, and state led development. Currently he is working on a book project on INTRACO, the former government linked company.

Gillian KOH is a Senior Research Fellow at the Institute of Policy Studies and contributes to the work in the Politics and Governance research cluster. Her on-going research interests lie in the areas of state-society relations, the development of civil society, and electoral politics in Singapore. She conducts surveys to track political attitudes of Singaporeans. She co-edited *"State-Society Relations in Singapore"* (2000) which is a book on the development of civil society here. She obtained a Bachelor of Arts degree (1988) from the National University of Singapore, a Master of Arts degree (1990) in Third World Studies at the Department of Sociological Studies, University of Sheffield, United Kingdom, and a PhD in Sociological Studies from the same department in 1995. She is a Director of the Social Enterprise Association (Singapore), Secretary of Social Venture Partners (Singapore) and a member of the Community Engagement Programme (Arts and Media Cluster).

Janadas Devan is Director of the Institute of Policy Studies and Associate Editor of *The Straits Times*, was educated at the National University of Singapore and Cornell University in the United States. He taught English in various institutions in Singapore and the US, and later wrote for various publications in the region, before joining *The Straits Times* in 1997. He served as the paper's leader writer for many years, writing unsigned editorials on a wide variety of subjects; wrote a weekly column on politics and economics, in which he covered international and domestic developments; a column on language for *The Sunday Times*; and since 2008, edited the paper's opinion pages. He also did a weekly radio broadcast, "Call from America," for Radio Singapore International, from 2000 to

2008, on American life and society. In 1988, he received the Clark Distinguished Teaching Award from Cornell University.

KOK Heng Leun, is Artistic Director of Drama Box Ltd, as is one of Singapore's few effectively bilingual theatre practitioners. He has extensive years of experience both in English and Mandarin productions, directing close to 60 plays. Under his helm, Drama Box has become known for its exciting theatrical works that are staged at major theatre venues and community housing estates. These works often address social issues that are relevant to Singapore society. He is also recognized as one of Singapore's major community theatre artists and has been invited to give papers and conducted community theatre workshops in Singapore and overseas conferences. To date, he has directed *Spirits Play* (Singapore 2009, India Delhi, 2010), *Drift* (2007, 2008, 2009), *Trick or Threat!* (2007–2010, Singapore and Austria), *A Stranger at Home* (2006), *HAPPY* (2005), *Liao Zhai* (2004), *Freedom From Toil* (Bangalore, India 2003); *Cloud Nine; Fugitives; White Songs* (2002 and 2001); *Have You Beaten?; Have You Eaten?; News Theatre; Mr Beng* (2000 and 1999); *Sang Nila* (International Puppet Festival, Vienna 1999); *Sour Relationship; Leng-Geh-Mng; Hazy Love* (1997; *Invisibility* (The Necessary Stage, Taipei 1997, Singapore 1996); and *Galileo —I Feel the Earth Move* (The Necessary Stage). Apart from his earlier works, Heng Leun has also collaborated with other playwrights to co-write *Drift; Trick or Threat; Soil* and *Tomorrow*. Plays he has adapted include: *A Stranger at Home; HAPPY; Liao Zhai* and *MoMo*. He has been dramaturgy for the Full Frontal series by the Singapore Arts Festival since 2007 and for Invisible Room, in collaboration with The Observatory and Ho Tzu Nyen (Singpaore 2009, and Germany 2010). He also curated a major festival about history of Singapore Chinese Language Theatre in 2010 at the Huayi Festival called *Scenes: Singapore Chinese Language Theatre*. He has co-edited a collection of contemporary Singapore Chinese Language plays and also co-wrote *Hey, There is play in the Classroom!*, the first book was entitled "*Drama in Education in Chinese Lanugage Learning in Singapore.*" Heng Leun was the recipient of the Young Artist Award in 2000 from the National Arts Council, Culture Award in 2003 from the Japanese Chamber of Commerce and Industry and the Outstanding Young Person of Singapore Award in 2006.

LAI Ah Eng is a Senior Research Fellow (Asian Migration Cluster) at the Asia Research Institute, National University of Singapore. She received training in economics at the University Sains Malaysia (1977), development studies at the Institute of Development Studies, Sussex (1981) and social anthropology at Cambridge University, 1992. She has worked in various research capacities at the Consumers' Association of Penang in Malaysia and at the Housing and Development Board, National Archives of Singapore, Institute of Southeast Asian Studies, and Institute of Policy Studies in Singapore. She also taught briefly at the Department of Economics, Universiti Sains Malaysia, and the Departments of Sociology and Social Work, National University of Singapore. Her research areas and publications cover issues of family and gender; migration, multiculturalism, ethnicity and religion; and local histories and heritages.

LIM Boon Heng is Deputy Chairman of People's Association and also served as Minister in the Prime Minister's Office until 2011. He joined Neptune Orient Lines after graduating from the University of Newcastle-upon-Tyne in 1970 with a BSc (Hons) degree in Naval Architecture. In 1980 he was elected Member of Parliament (MP) for Kebun Baru and served there for three terms. In 1991, he was elected as MP for Ulu Pandan, and re-elected when Ulu Pandan became part of the Bukit Timah GRC in 1997. Since 2001, he has been the MP for Jurong GRC. Mr Lim's trade union career began in 1981 where he rose from the rank of Assistant Secretary-General in 1983 to become the Secretary-General of NTUC in 1993, stepping down at the end of 2006. Mr Lim also held several appointments: Chairman of the Ang Mo Kio West Town Council (1986–1991), Deputy Speaker of Parliament (1989–1991) and Chairman of National Productivity Board (1991–2003). He was appointed Senior Minister of State for Trade and Industry in 1991. In 1993, he was appointed Second Minister for Trade and Industry concurrently holding the post of Minister in the Prime Minister's Office. In 1997, he was re-appointed Minister without Portfolio. In 2001 and 2006, he was appointed Minister in the Prime Minister's Office.

In April 2011, Mr Lim announced that he would be retiring from politics and would not seek re-election in the 2011 Singapore General Election.

Sylvia LIM completed her undergraduate studies at NUS and her postgraduate studies in London. She was called to the Singapore Bar in 1991. Having a keen interest in criminal justice and social issues, she joined the Police Force as an Inspector for 3 years and expended energies in investigation work at Central Police Division and was also a staff officer to Director, Criminal Investigation Department. She returned to practice law in 1994 and was engaged in litigation work in both civil and criminal matters. In 1998, she joined Temasek Polytechnic as a law lecturer. She was later took over as a Manager of Professional Development at the Polytechnic's Business School, overseeing the training of adult learners. Her preferred areas of teaching and writing are in civil and criminal procedure, criminal justice and private security. Sylvia has been Chairman of the Workers' Party since June 2003. She became a Non-Constituency Member of Parliament (NCMP) after leading a Workers' Party team to contest Aljunied GRC in the 2006 General Elections and securing 43.9% of the votes cast. In her capacity as NCMP since 2006, she was active in Parliamentary debates on diverse topics and also contributed to the review of legislation particularly in the area of criminal justice.

In the 2011 General Election, Ms Lim was part of the Workers' Party team contesting in Aljunied GRC and beat the PAP with 54.7% of votes. After winning the election, Ms Lim announced her resignation from Temasek Polytechnic in May 2011.

ONG Keng Yong — On July 2011, Mr. Ong relinquished his post as Director of the Institute of Policy Studies and his concurrent appointments as Ambassador-At-Large in the Singapore Ministry of Foreign Affairs and Singapore's Non-Resident Ambassador to Iran to become Singapore's High Commissioner to Malaysia. He was Secretary-General of ASEAN (Association of Southeast Asian Nations) from January 2003 to January 2008. His earlier diplomatic postings took him to Saudi Arabia, Malaysia, and the USA. He was Singapore's Ambassador to India and Nepal from 1996 to 1998. He was appointed Press Secretary to the Prime Minister of

Singapore and concurrently held senior positions in the Ministry of Information, Communications and the Arts, and the People's Association in Singapore from 1998 to 2002. He is a graduate of the University of Singapore and Georgetown University (Washington DC, USA).

ONG Ye Kung is the Assistant Secretary-General of National Trades Union Congress (NTUC). He oversees the Labour Movement's employment and employability programmes and initiatives which include serving as the Chairman of Employment and Employability Institute Pte Ltd (e2i). He also holds the positions of Executive Secretary in the National Transport Workers Union (NTWU) and Singapore Manual and Mercantile Workers' Union (SMMWU). Prior to joining NTUC, he was the Chief Executive of Singapore Workforce Development Agency (WDA). He spearheaded many initiatives to build up the Continuing Education and Training infrastructure for Singapore, and made training accessible to the individual worker, including contract workers and the unemployed. Mr Ong sits on the Boards of SPRING Singapore, SMRT Corporation Ltd, JTC Corporation, Chinese Development Assistance Council (CDAC), NTUC Investment Co-operative Ltd (NIC) and NTUC LearningHub Pte Ltd (LHUB). He also serves on the Board of Governors of Northlight School. He is a member of Ngee Ann Polytechnic Council, a Trustee of the Singapore LSE Trust and Chairman of Workers' Upgrading and Employment Committee of Chinese Development Assistance Council. Mr Ong has a First Class Honours in B.Sc (Economics) from the University of London, London School of Economics and Political Science (UK) and a Master of Business Administration from the Institute of Management Development, Lausanne, Switzerland.

In February 2011, Mr Ong left the administrative service to contest as candidate in the PAP team for Aljunied, where they were outpolled by the Workers' Party in the 2011 General Election. Following the election, Mr Ong was appointed Deputy Secretary General of NTUC.

Ori SASSON is the founder and CEO of Simulation Software & Technology (S2T), a Singapore-based company focusing on training, simulation, and knowledge management systems. Under his leadership, S2T has grown from a one-man company to employ over 50 engineers over the span of eight years. In addition to S2T, he also founded Dynamics Speech, which is the largest private speech therapy practice in Singapore, and Dynamics Success Centre, an occupational therapy practice, both of which serve a large number of children with special needs. He earned his PhD in Computer Science from the Hebrew University of Jerusalem in Israel in 2006 and is the author of several research papers in diverse fields ranging from Theoretical Computer Science and Bioinformatics to Simulation and Innovation Management. He has also co-authored five technical books on technologies to build enterprise business solutions. Ori is a Singapore citizen and lives in Singapore with his wife and two Singapore-born sons.

Denise PHUA Lay Peng is a Singaporean politician and active volunteer and advocate for the special needs community. After a successful corporate career spanning two decades, she was elected as President of the not-for-profit charity, Autism Resource Centre (Singapore). She co-founded Pathlight School, the first autism school in Singapore and currently oversees two special schools and all services in two charities. She is also a Member of Parliament (MP), representing the ruling People's Action Party (PAP) in Jalan Besar Group Representation Constituency. As an MP, she has focused on advocating for the disabled and special needs communities in Singapore, especially those from poor and needy backgrounds. She is one of the key architects of Singapore's latest five-year (2007–2011) Enabling Master Plan which charts services and programmes for the disabled.

T. Sasitharan (Sasi) is co-founder and director of the Theatre Training and Research Programme (TTRP), a theatre conservatory which runs a three-year, full-time training course for professional actors. It is the only programme in the world offering systematic training in contemporary acting. Together with the late Kuo Pao Kun, Sasi conceived and established TTRP in August 2000. TTRP is also one of the founding members of the independent arts social enterprise, Emily Hill. Sasi was Artistic Director of The Substation from April 1995 to August 2000. A writer and commentator, he has had articles ranging from commentaries on culture and the arts to reviews of performances, exhibitions, talks and catalogue entries published in Singapore and abroad. He is frequently invited to speak at conferences on arts, education, and creativity, most notably as a keynote speaker for the World Summit on Arts and Culture 2009 in Johannesburg, South Africa. One of Singapore's most respected actors; he has worked with directors like Pao Kun, Kishen Jit, Max le Blond, and Chandra Lingam.

T. Raja SEGAR has been Chief Executive Officer of the Singapore Indian Development Association (SINDA) since December 2009, after joining the organisation as Senior Director in June 2008 and being promoted a year later as Chief Operating Officer in June 2009.

A trained teacher, he started his career as an Economics teacher in a government school, before joining a private education company as the Head of Management Studies. Later, he joined Nanyang Polytechnic as a Lecturer of Economics. Called to launch the Indian programme belt, Vasantham Central, on the local television channel *Central*, he stayed with Mediacorp for about three years before joining the Institute of Technical Education as a Course Manager of Business Studies. Prior to joining SINDA, he was Head of Education and Career Transition at MINDEF. He holds a Masters in Finance from RMIT, a Bachelor of Science Degree in Economics from NUS and a Diploma in Education from NTU. His interests include computers, philosophy, performing arts, and education management.

T. K. UDAIRAM is currently the Chief Executive Officer of Changi General Hospital, an 800-bed acute care hospital, and is also Chairman of Mercy Relief. He has 34 years of experience in healthcare operations, administration and management, having held various posts in several public hospitals and the Ministry of Health. Udairam was involved in the planning and successful implementation of the Medisave Scheme, the national healthcare financing scheme in 1983–1984. As Administrator at Singapore General Hospital, he was also involved with the restructuring of the hospital from a government department. He went on in 1993 to commission the Ang Mo Kio Community Hospital. In 2000, he was appointed the CEO of Changi General Hospital, which he established as an energy-efficient and pro-environment hospital. Under his helm, Changi General Hospital has also become a leader in developing electronic services to improve productivity and speed of hospital processes and is currently engaged in developing systems and processes to improve the health of the community in the East.

WONG Kan Seng served as Singapore's Deputy Prime Minister from 2005 to 2011 and Coordinating Minister for National Security from 2010 to 2011. He graduated with a Bachelor of Arts (Honours) degree in 1970 from the then University of Singapore and a Master of Science degree from the London Business School in 1979 on a Singapore Government scholarship. After leaving secondary school, he taught for three years before pursuing further studies at the University of Singapore. He joined the Administrative Service in 1970. He had worked in the then Ministry of Labour and the Ministry of Defence (MINDEF). He held appointments as a Department Head of the Republic of Singapore Navy, Director of Manpower Division and the Deputy Secretary till 1981 when he left to join Hewlett Packard, Singapore where he remained till January 1985. He first contested and won the 1984 Parliamentary election as the People's Action Party candidate for the Kuo Chuan Constituency in Toa Payoh. Since then, he has been re-elected as Member of Parliament in six successive general elections. In February 1985, Mr Wong was appointed Minister of State for Home Affairs, briefly and for Community Development, and Communications and Information. In 1986, he was appointed the acting Minister for Community Development and Minister of State for Communications and Information. In 1987, Mr Wong became the Minister for Community Development, a position he held till 1991. He was also appointed as the Leader of the House (Parliament) in 1987 and held that position till March 2007. He was also concurrently the Second Minister for Foreign Affairs, and became the Minister for Foreign Affairs in 1988. He was appointed the Home Affairs Minister in 1994, and promoted as Deputy Prime Minister on 1 September 2005. As Home Affairs Minister, Mr Wong chaired a number of ministerial-level committees which coordinated work across several ministries, for example, on crisis management and community engagement. As Deputy Prime Minister, he oversaw the National Population Secretariat and chaired the National Population Committee. On 1 November 2010, Mr Wong relinquished his appointment as Minister for Home Affairs and became the Coordinating Minister for National Security. Mr Wong was the Deputy Chairman of the People's Association for 15 years from 1992 to 2006. Apart from appointments in the Government, Mr Wong is the Adviser of the National Transport Workers' Union since 1985. He was the Chairman of the

Chinese Development Assistance Council from 1992 to 2004. He is a member of the London Business School's Global Advisory Council. Mr Wong has been a member of the People's Action Party's Central Executive Committee since 1987 and was its Second Assistant Secretary-General from 1992 to 2004 when he became its First Assistant Secretary-General till May 2011. He is now a member of the People's Action Party Central Executive Committee. For his contributions to the Civil Service and Labour Movement, Mr Wong was awarded the Public Administration Medal (Silver) in 1976 and the National Trade Union Congress May Day Medal of Honour in 1998. He received the London Business School Alumni Achievement Award in 2004.

Mr Wong stepped down from his position as Deputy Prime Minister and Coordinating Minister for National Security in May 2011 and continues to serve as a Member of Parliament representing the Bishan-Toa Payoh GRC.

Woffles WU has been the medical director and consultant aesthetic and plastic surgeon at the Woffles Wu Aesthetic Surgery and Laser Centre Singapore since 2000. He graduated with a MBBS from the National University of Singapore in 1984 and qualified as a surgeon with the Royal College of Surgeons of Edinburgh, UK, in 1989 before being board-certified by the Academy of Medicine, Singapore, in plastic surgery in 1994. He is not only a member of but also sits on numerous committees in several international professional bodies such as the International Society of Aesthetic Plastic Surgeons ISAPS, the International Consortium of Aesthetic Plastic Surgeons ICAPS and the American Society of Aesthetic Plastic Surgeons ASAPS. In 2005, he served as the Vice Chairman of the International Association of Aesthetic Plastic Surgeons IAAPS. He has also written chapters for medical books including AO/ASIF Craniomaxillofacial Course Handbook and Textbook of Clinical Trials (2nd edition) and has shared his experience in over 100 international conferences and symposia where he has been an invited keynote speaker, panelist, or moderator. He pioneered the Stealth Incision Technique for scarless breast augmentation in 1996 which is used by Plastic surgeons all around the world and developed the Woffles Thread and Woffles Lift non-surgical facelifting procedure in 2002. He has been featured on television and in over 250 books, newspaper, and magazine articles for his outstanding career in cosmetic surgery, including as one of the 20 most famous plastic surgeons in the world in the 2006 book "Aesthetic Surgery" published by Taschen Books. He is the Honorary Head of Department of the Department of Plastic Surgery at the Zhejiang Peoples Hospital in Hangzhou, China. He is a member of the Malay Heritage Committee and the Oral Archives Committee of the National Heritage Board NHB, sits on the Public Sculpture Appraisal Committee of the NHB and is a member of the Singapore Film Commission.

He is known for his philanthropic contributions to the National University of Singapore as well as St Andrew's Village and is the current President of the St Andrew's Alumni Association.

Aside from being a former national ten-pin bowler and snooker player, he also maintains a keen interest in the arts. His paintings have been exhibited in Singapore and Taiwan, and he has acted in film, on TV and the stage. In 2004, he appeared in both The Necessary Stage's comedy, *Starlight*, and jazz diva Jacintha's sell out stage show. An avid cinephile, he was the Executuve Producer and Co-Producer of the 2006 hit feature film *Singapore Dreaming* which won Best Screenplay Award at the 2006 San Sebastian Film Festival and Best Asian Film Award at the Tokyo International Film Festival 2007. He recently danced live on the President's Star Charity 2007 and continues to raise funds for *The Straits Times School Pocket Money Fund*. He also conducts volunteer medical missions to the underprivileged destinations within Asia and Southeast Asia.

About the Institute of Policy Studies

The Institute of Policy Studies (IPS) was established in 1988 to promote a greater awareness of policy issues and good governance. Today, IPS is a think-tank within the Lee Kuan Yew School of Public Policy at the National University of Singapore. It seeks to cultivate clarity of thought, forward thinking and a big-picture perspective on issues of critical national interest through strategic deliberation and research. It adopts a multi-disciplinary approach in its analysis and takes the long-term view. It studies the attitudes and aspirations of Singaporeans which have an impact on policy development and the relevant areas of diplomacy and international affairs. The Institute bridges and engages the diverse stakeholders through its conferences and seminars, closed-door discussions, publications, and surveys on public perceptions of policy.